The Twist

The Twist

The Story of the
Song and Dance
That Changed the World

Jim Dawson

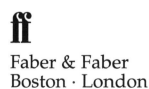

Faber & Faber
Boston · London

All rights reserved under International and Pan-American Copyright
Conventions, including the right of reproduction in whole or in part
in any form. First published in the United States in 1995 by
Faber and Faber, Inc., 50 Cross Street, Winchester, MA 01890.

Cataloging-in-Publication Data for this book
is available from the Library of Congress.

ISBN 0 571 19852 X

Cover design by Mary Maurer
Cover photo of Chubby Checker courtesy Michael Ochs Archives, Ltd.
Printed in the United States of America

Dedication

Where were you in '62? If you were alive,
you were doin' the Twist!

To Hank Ballard, who started more than just the Twist.
And to the beautiful memory of Tina Tei, who taught me how.

Contents

Acknowledgments

I would like to thank the Academy of Motion Picture Arts and Sciences, Dave Appell, Hank Ballard, Robin Banks, Richard Berry, John Broven, Louise Bruce, Trevor Cajiao, Ray Campi, Freddy Cannon, Little Joe Cook, Joey Dee, Aaron Fuchs, Ray Funk, Bill Gardner, Galen Gart, Charlie Gracie, Cal Green, the late Rene Hall, Gladys Horton, Wayne Jancik, Wayne Jones, Kitty Karp, John Medora, Kal Mann, Ron Mann, the late Krazy Greg Milewski, Harry Narunsky, the Michael Ochs Archives, Earl Palmer, Steve and Sylvia Propes, Robert Pruter, Pete Ricci, Jeff Riley, Bobby Robinson, Chuck Rubin of Artists Rights Enforcement Corporation, Dee Dee Sharp, Phil Spector, Veronica Spector, John Stalberg, Mike Stark, Joe Tarsia, Triton Pictures, my editor Betsy Uhrig, Billy Vera, Brother Joseph Wallace, Brian Walsh, my agent Frank Weimann, Richard Weize, Sir Ian Whitcomb, David White, Tony Wilkinson, and Joe Wissert for their invaluable recollections, assistance, and/or encouragement.

Introduction

twist (twĭst) *v.* twisted, twisting, twists.—*intr.* To squirm,
writhe. To rotate or revolve. *n.* The act of twisting or the
condition of being twisted; a spin or twirl; rotation."
—The American Heritage Dictionary

There are no basic steps to the Twist. You move chest, hips
and arms from side to side and balance on the balls of
your feet."
—Chubby Checker

The sixties didn't mathematically begin until New Year's Day,
1961, but the American mania for putting bookends on decades
and labeling them, as if each ten-year increment were a separate
and distinct epoch, includes an insistence upon beginning each
decade with a zero, and so we think of 1960 not as the last year
of the fifties (which it was) but as the first of the sixties. In some
ways this tidiness makes sense. Nineteen-sixty did seem like
the beginning of the youthful and rebellious sixties, when the
boom babies of the late forties earnestly frolicked through their
teenage years. It was in 1960 that Pepsi-Cola came up with the
sixties' slogan, "For Those Who Think Young." It was the year
America elected a young president. And it was the first full-on
year of the Twist, the uninhibited dance that challenged the val-
ues and authority of the Depression generation and set into
motion a new body language that we continue to carry with us
today.

Chubby Checker's recording of "The Twist" is the only
nonholiday single ever to go to number one on the Hit Parade
(in 1960), drop completely off the charts, and then, in a new
burst of popularity, rise all the way to number one a second

time (in 1962). (Bing Crosby's perennial "White Christmas" reached pop heaven three times, in 1942, 1945, and 1946.) "The Twist" occupied *Billboard*'s Top Forty for a combined thirty-three weeks, longer at the time than any other record except, again, Crosby's "White Christmas." Even today, people all over the world still remember—or have seen in film clips—Chubby Checker singing and dancing to "The Twist." At a time when the United States was patenting the laser, circumnavigating the Earth underwater with a nuclear submarine, launching the first weather satellites, and orbiting its first men in space (all between early 1960 and mid-1962), the Twist was something sleek and modern and space-age. For Americans, giddy with prosperity and the promise of a brave new future, the Twist seemed part of the overall exhilaration, sending everyone 'round and around and around and around.

"The Twist" was an echo of the mid-fifties rock and roll revolution, which by 1960 had limped into an inglorious dead period of overgroomed whelps whining and whimpering along with prerecorded instrumental tracks. But whereas rock and roll jumped to the beat, "The Twist" glided on the rhythm. The forces that had appropriated and tamed rock and roll—the Mafia, Madison Avenue, television impresarios, and aging record-company and music-publishing executives—were in position to exploit the Twist craze by making it rock and roll's replacement. Checker's "The Twist" was in fact a chord-for-chord mimicry of an earlier, rawer recording of "The Twist" by rock and roll pioneer Hank Ballard.

"The Twist" accomplished during its three-year run what rock and roll never did: It assimilated. It hid its uncouth roots, ascended to the middle class, and even prospered as slumming music for the glittering and chattering classes. The Twist phenomenon was the older generation's coming to terms with rock and roll, albeit six or seven years late; it was also a bellwether for the rise of a more mechanical and middlebrow form of rock and roll in the mid-sixties.

Besides being the only dance to cross the modern generation gap, the Twist changed the way Americans danced. It broke away not only from the rules of leading and following—it broke all rules! And it set off a string of copycat dances—the Hully Gully, the Pony, the Frug, the Monkey, the Mashed Potatoes, and any number of other gyrations and twitches not seen since the medieval St. Vitus Stomp—that urged people, particularly whites, to forget the comportment they'd inherited from European ballrooms and "express themselves" (a fatuous sixties mantra if ever there was one) with their bodies on the dance floor. As their dancing became more uninhibited, it created a kind of mass possession, a mild frenzy that brought relief and release from self-absorption. At the same time, these dances, despite their standard of physical separation between partners, bonded them together with a tribal immediacy. They also provided a way for dancers to flaunt the era's restrictive sexual codes, and in that regard the Twist and its many variations helped set in motion the nation's musical, social, cultural, and political upheavals of the later sixties.

This is the story of "The Twist". . . and the Twist.

1: Hey, Let's Twist!

> "On the ballroom floor you allow liberties to men that you never allow them elsewhere. You grant them liberties on the ballroom floor that if a man other than your husband would attempt them in your home and your husband would find you at it, he would have no trouble in securing a divorce, and if he shot the man no jury in the world would convict him for it."
> —Reverend Billy Sunday, protesting the tango, 1915

> "Do not wriggle the shoulders. Do not shake the hips. Do not twist the body."
> —1920s advertisement for the Vernon and Irene Castle Dance Studio

There was nothing new about the Twist as a name for a dance or as a dance itself—or, for that matter, even as a song. There was the "French twist"—a movement within the high-kicking, nineteenth-century dance-hall routine called the cancan. The dancers, facing the audience with their hands in front of their crotches, kicked one leg straight out to one side and then kicked the other leg to the opposite side. (Groucho Marx performed this step in a couple of films.) And then there was a pelvic dance motion called the "twist" that, according to Marshall and Jean Stearns, authors of *Jazz Dance,* came to America from the Congo during slavery. The earliest documentation of this form is a playbill for an American minstrel show called *Dandy Jim from Caroline,* starring the legendary black Virginia Minstrels, touring Scotland and England in 1844. While banjoist Dan Emmett plucked a tune called "Grape Vine Twist," his partners Richard Pelham and Frank Brower—sketched on the playbill wearing sparrow-cut suits, with their legs spread and arms outstretched at a forty-five-degree angle to their bodies—did something

1

called "grapevine twisting." Exactly what this twist consisted of is no longer known.

The first African-based dance craze swept white America in the latter part of the nineteenth century. It had begun on southern plantations where, during the harvest celebrations, slaves vied for prizes, usually large cakes, by spoofing European dances with hyperelegant, high-stepping struts and eurythmic prances. After the Civil War, minstrel performers standardized these elaborate steps into what was commonly called the Cakewalk. As its popularity spread, composers wrote songs for it, such as "Walking for Dat Cake" (1877), a highlight of the popular burlesque show, *Mulligan Guard.* Within ten years there were dozens of songs celebrating the Cakewalk, and many more — including the military-style marches of John Philip Sousa — that used the Cakewalk's buoyant syncopations. (Thanks to Sousa, the Cakewalk survives today on football fields in the arched-back swagger of baton-twirling majorettes.)

In 1912, black composer Perry Bradford wrote a faux ragtime song called "Messin' Around" in which he described a new dance called the Mess Around: "Now anybody can learn the knack, put your hands on your hips and bend your back; stand in one spot nice and tight, and twist around, twist around with all your might." The twist Bradford described was a swirling or rotating of the hips and buttocks in a rough imitation of sexual intercourse. Most likely he picked it up from an earlier source. Bert Williams, the first black superstar of vaudeville and silent films, as well as a popular songwriter who worked the same African-based musical territory as Bradford, wrote before his death in 1922 that "it would be more correct to say that I assembled [songs]. For the tunes to popular songs are mostly made up of standard parts, like a motor car." In turn, some of the melody and lyrics of "Messin' Around" would be borrowed seventeen years later by blues pianist Clarence "Pine Top" Smith for his 1929 pop hit, "Pine Top's Boogie Woogie" — the first record with "boogie woogie" in the title. That same year, on another variation of "Messin' Around" called "Fat Fanny Stomp," pianist Jim Clark sang: "Aw, shake your fat fanny, I mean shake your ol' fanny, twirl that thing, gal, twirl it, wring it, twist it a little bit!" Nearly twenty-five years after that, Ray Charles stumbled onto the R&B charts with an updated "Mess Around." (Chubby Checker would record a Twist song called "Dance the Mess Around" in 1961, but it had nothing to do with the original song beyond the title.)

In 1913, less than a year after the introduction of "Messin' Around," two black Tin Pan Alleymen, Chris Smith and Jim Burris, borrowed the hula-like pelvic roll of the Mess Around in a song called "Ballin' the Jack." Lyricist Burris subverted the foxtrot rhythm of "Ballin' the Jack" by instructing dancers to do something quite unlike the foxtrot: "First you put your two knees close up tight, then you sway 'em to the left, then you sway 'em to the right; step around the floor kind of nice and light, then you twist around and twist around with all of your might." After it debuted in *The Darktown Follies of 1913* at Harlem's Lafayette Theater, "Ballin' the Jack" became such a hot tune among the society swells slipping uptown to eddy their midsections that impresario Florenz Ziegfeld, who had been staging wildly popular musical revues since 1907, put the song into his *Ziegfeld's Follies* at the palatial New Amsterdam Theater on Forty-second Street, just off Times Square. The Ballin' the Jack dance craze culminated in a number-one (for three weeks) platter, "Ballin' the Jack," by Charles Prince's all-white orchestra in late 1914. Although white Americans had been recycling African dance steps since before the turn of the century, Ballin' the Jack was the first to become nationally vogue. (Chubby Checker recorded an updated but faithful "Ballin' the Jack" in 1962.)

Ballin' the Jack was followed in the mid-1920s by the Black Bottom, complete, naturally, with a hit song called "Black Bottom," billing itself in the lyrics as "a new twister." As with the earlier black dances, the essence of the Black Bottom was a shaking and thrusting of the hips and buttocks, at least when performed by blacks. But as these dances crossed over into the Jazz Age's white society, they lost much of their sexual suggestiveness. Whites still danced under the sway of European decorum: body erect, moving only the shoulders and feet. Rolling or rotating the hips and bending the knees—"getting down"—were considered vulgar.

By 1928 there were at least three more songs about the twist: The New Orleans Owls recorded "New Twister"; another group waxed "The Baltimore," whose lyrics promoted "That new twister called the Baltimore"; most significantly, when Duke Ellington signed with OKeh Records and rerecorded his radio theme song, which had been released originally on Vocalion in 1926 as "East St. Louis Toodle-Oo," the company issued it as "Harlem Twist." The following year, Ferdinand "Jelly Roll" Morton, one of the fathers of jazz, waxed "Turtle Twist" for Victor. The sexual implications of the word "twist" became more overt in a song called "Winin' Boy Blues," recorded by Morton at least five times for five different labels between 1938 and 1940, though it originates from earlier sources. The lyric—"Mama, mama, look at sis, she's out on the levee doin' the double twist"—referred to a whore working the docks. In 1947, black Chicago saxophonist Buster Bennett echoed Morton's song in a jump blues called "I Want to Boogie Woogie," shouting, "Mama, mama, look at sis, she's out in the backyard trying to do the twist, she wants to boogie." (Boogie, which possibly came from the West African word *buga*, to beat, was also a euphemism for sexual intercourse, among other things.) A year later, baritone saxophonist Paul Williams warmed up for his million-selling "The Hucklebuck" by recording "The Twister," an R&B instrumental hit. Out on the West Coast, R&B combo leader Roy Milton recorded a guitar-driven instrumental called "T-Town Twist," whose rhythm easily would have propelled Twisters more than a decade later.

Even during the 1950s the twist kept popping up in rhythm and blues lyrics. For example, a Clyde McPhatter and the Drifters recording from 1953 (though not released until 1960) called

"Let the Boogie Woogie Roll" contained the line: "When she looked at me her eyes just shined like gold, and when she did the twist she bopped me to my soul." Richard Berry, who later wrote and recorded the original "Louie Louie," mentioned the twist in a 1956 song he wrote for Etta James called "Good Rockin' Daddy": "They stood around with a great big smile, and when you did the crazy twist they all went wild." These records, incidentally, referred to the boogie as a dance, implying that the twist was a part of doing the boogie.

When asked recently about that line, Berry said he had only a vague memory of what he meant by the twist. "It was a form of dancing. In those days you had two dances—the Scrunch, where you stood in one spot and did the grind with your girl, or you did a fast dance where you did everything. They had so many dances back then that didn't have any names. I guess that was the twist."

Although it would be enough to say that the song we now know as "The Twist" has its roots in "Messin' Around," we can go one better and trace its genealogy directly to North Carolina in the 1930s. "It was something I heard my sister doing back in Williamston when I was a boy," Brother Joseph "Jo Jo" Wallace, a longtime member of a successful gospel recording group called the Sensational Nightingales, said from his Durham home in 1988. "They'd sing, 'Twist . . . twist' while they were playing, and it always stuck with me. Me and another fellow in the group, Bill Woodruff, started having fun with it [many years later]. I put a beat to it with my little guitar and we came up with, 'Come on, baby, let's do the twist, who taught you how to do the twist?' But then we kinda took it off in another direction. The tune was different." Wallace himself never recorded the song. He said a third member of the Sensational Nightingales, David Edwinton, later passed the song on to Hank Ballard, leader of a popular rhythm and blues group called the Midnighters. (Wallace's recollection that his opening line was "Come on, baby, let's do the twist" may be flawed; Hank Ballard's original demo of "The Twist" had a different opening lyric—

but more on that later.) When pressed to sing his original version of "The Twist," Brother Joseph Wallace delivered a ram-
bling fifteen-bar blues that bore only a passing resemblance to
the later hit. But as Hank Ballard himself admitted, it was the
germ of the song.

2: Twist with Me, Henry

"They call Chubby the father of the Twist, but he's
just the stepfather. I'm the father. It's my baby."
—Hank Ballard

Henry "Hank" Ballard is a small, dark, wiry man with a large
head and an infectious laugh that he uses to punctuate his sen-
tences. As he approaches sixty, Ballard does not look all that different from the photos of the athletic young lion who electrified
rhythm and blues music in the 1950s. Hank Ballard is one of
those guys whom older black musicians call a "singingest cat"
because he's always singing a line here, a line there; always
ready to fill out an anecdote with a few finger pops and a snatch
of an old tune. When he tells you that one of his boyhood idols
was singing cowboy Gene Autry, he caps it with a few lines
from "Back in the Saddle Again," and as he talks about another
influence, Jimmy Rushing from the Count Basie Band, he'll toss
in a fair baritone imitation of Rushing shouting, "Got a mind to
ramble, got a mind to go home, got a mind to be a good boy,
leave all you bad women alone," then slip into another laugh.

Hank Ballard was born John Henry Kendricks in Detroit on
November 18, 1936, and lost his parents early. "I didn't know
my full, real name until the army wanted to see a birth certifi-
cate," he says. "I went to live with my aunt in Bessemer, Ala-
bama, when I was a little boy, but I returned to Michigan when
I was thirteen. Ran away, didn't like the South at all. Soon as I
turned sixteen I got a job working on the line at Ford Motor
Company." Despite the steady paycheck and the grown-up in-
dependence that his job provided him, Hank yearned for the
glamorous if unpredictable life of black show business. "I loved
the gospel groups like the Dixie Hummingbirds, and I loved the

7

Orioles, the Ink Spots, the Ravens—[tries to sing in a Maithe Marshall-high tenor voice] 'Marie, the dawn is breaking.' My idol was Clyde McPhatter, wasn't nobody like Clyde McPhatter—[sings] 'Have mercy, mercy, baby.' Soon as I heard him, I knew I had to sing." His dream took shape when he met a coworker named Sonny Woods. "He worked on the line with me, and he'd hear me singing. One day he asked me if I'd like to audition for his group."

A couple of years earlier, Sonny Woods had been a utility man, valet and fill-in bass singer for the Orioles, a seminal rhythm and blues vocal group whose 1948 recording of "It's Too Soon to Know" had crossed over into the high regions of the pop charts. When their charismatic lead singer, Sonny Til, stopped touring and the Orioles began to break up, Woods returned home to Detroit and recruited three friends—lead tenor Henry Booth, baritone-tenor Charles Sutton, and baritone Lawson Smith—to form a new group called the Royals. Not long afterward, in late 1951, Los Angeles bandleader Johnny Otis caught their performance at an amateur show at Detroit's Paradise Theater and put them in touch with Ralph Bass, the head of Federal Records, a subsidiary of King Records in Cincinnati. The Royals recorded their first session in January 1952. Their debut single was a solid Johnny Otis tune called "Every Beat of My Heart," but the Royals' version, far too lugubrious for its own good, suffered congestive failure. The song wouldn't be hit-worthy until Gladys Knight and the Pips recorded it a few years later.

When Hank Ballard replaced Lawson Smith in the group and took over the lead vocal duties from Henry Booth in early 1953, he brought along his penchant for writing catchy, explicit lyrics. At his first session, in May, he recorded an original song, "Get It," that left no doubt what he was singing about: "C'mon and get it, get it, get it . . . You know I wanna see you wit' it." "Get It" became the Royals' first rhythm and blues chart record. But the dirty ditty that put the group in the big time was Ballard's "Work with Me, Annie," the top-selling rhythm and blues hit of 1954 and one of the most influential recordings of its time, despite being denounced as "smut" by *Billboard* and *Variety* and blacklisted by dozens of black radio stations, including Memphis's powerhouse WDIA, which considered such lyrics as "Annie, please don't cheat, give me all my meat!" too profane for airplay. "Work with Me, Annie" not only established Ballard as a major talent but gave him a lesson about songwriting: If something works once, there's a good chance it'll work again. He recorded at least three "Annie" sequels, including "Annie Had a Baby" (also a number-one R&B hit) and "Annie's Aunt Fanny" (a Top Ten R&B hit), that shared the basic melody and structure of "Work with Me, Annie," as if each record was simply a movement, or chapter, within a larger composition. Ballard's willingness to reuse a melody until he'd wrung every note and nuance from it would pay dividends a couple of years later with "The Twist."

Just as "Work with Me, Annie" was working up a sweat, King Records signed a jump blues vocal group called the 5 Royales. Clearly the 5 Royales and the Royals couldn't coexist in the same King/Federal stable without creating some confusion for the distributors and fans. Since the 5 Royales were already stars and the Royals were upstarts, Ballard and the guys changed their name to the Midnighters to match the after-hours image they cultivated on their records.

One of the hit answer records to Ballard's "Work with Me, Annie" was Etta James's "Roll with Me, Henry," featuring Richard Berry ("Hmm-hmm, baby") as the voice of Henry. During a 1956 sequel to "Roll with Me, Henry" called "Good Rockin' Daddy," Etta James referred to Henry "doin' the crazy twist." Was this just a coincidence? Apparently so, because that same year the Sensational Nightingales's Brother Joseph Wallace had only begun to shop his song, "The Twist," to other artists. One was a young South Philadelphia singer named Joe Cook, who, as Little Joe and the Thrillers, would later have a 1957 pop seller called "Peanuts." Cook claimed from his Boston home a few years ago that Wallace offered him the song first: "I was working with a gospel group from Philly, the Davis Sisters. I drove them down to Atlanta for a gospel show [in late 1956], and at the hotel room I ran into two guys who had been in the Evening Star Quartet with me a couple of years before. Now they were in a group called the [Sensational] Nightingales. They knew I'd had a hit with 'Let's Do the Slop' [for OKeh Records in 1954] and they gave me this dance song called 'Let's Do the Twist' that went, 'Come on, baby, let's do the twist.' It went 'up and down and around and around.' We put it on tape and I took it back to New York, but OKeh Records discouraged me from doing the song because it was too dirty." (Incidentally, Cook's "Slop"—"I made the dance up myself"—was one of Philadelphia's first homegrown dance steps.)

So Hank Ballard became the song's beneficiary. The Midnighters' guitarist, Cal Green, now a resident of Los Angeles, recalls: "We were in Tampa, Florida, and we were staying at the same hotel as a spiritual group, the [Sensational] Nightingales, and they idolized us. This guy had scribbled something on a piece of paper and brought it to Hank. He said, 'We can't record this, we're a spiritual group, see what you can do with it, you can have the song.' So Hank says, 'Get your guitar, Cal, let's see what we can do with it.' The melody was already there but it was a fifteen-bar blues so we changed it to twelve bars and changed some words around." According to Green, this exchange took place in 1957.

Earlier that year the Midnighters had recorded a song called "Is Your Love for Real?" Its writers are listed as Cal Green and Hank Ballard. But the melody sounds almost exactly like a 1955 rhythm and blues hit by Clyde McPhatter and the Drifters called "What'cha Gonna Do?"—and both Green and Ballard admitted that that's where they got the melody for "Is Your Love for Real?" (The credited songwriter of "What'cha Gonna Do?" is Ahmet Ertegun, the co-owner of Atlantic Records, but the song bears more than a passing resemblance to a 1953 gospel recording, also called "What'cha Gonna Do?," by the Radio Four on the small Republic label out of Tennessee.) Because

Ballard's success with "Work with Me, Annie" and its sequels had demonstrated that a popular melody should be used over and over until the public got sick of it, he recycled the tune of "What'cha Gonna Do?" and "Is Your Love for Real?" by grafting the lyrics of "The Twist" onto it.

While the band was playing at a Florida chain of chitlin circuit clubs called the Palms in the early spring of 1958, a Miami record producer named Henry Stone taped a demo of the Midnighters' new song, along with a ballad called "I'll Pray for You," in a high-school auditorium. Cal Green played a chord progression that he himself said "sounded like Jimmy Reed." The group's saxophonist blew a raw sixteen-bar solo. Ballard sent the tape to Vee-Jay Records, a black-owned company in Chicago, because his contract with Federal Records was ready to expire at the end of 1958 and he was flirting with other labels. Since the group hadn't had a hit in almost three years, he figured that Syd Nathan, president of King Records, would quietly drop them. But Nathan surprised Ballard at the last minute by exercising his option to renew the contract. In fact, he moved the Midnighters from Federal over to the parent label, where they would remain for the next ten years. Vee-Jay tossed Ballard's now-useless demo tape of "The Twist" and "I'll Pray for You" into a vault and forgot about it for the next thirty years.

On November 11, 1958, the Midnighters recorded "The Twist" again, this time in King's Cincinnati studio in the rear of Syd Nathan's factory building at 1540 Brewster Avenue, in the Evanston part of town. The vocal group was backed by veteran bandleader-pianist Alfonso "Sonny" Thompson's studio band: tenor saxists Ray Felder and James E. Moore, Edwyn Conley on standup bass, Havarre Hastings on Fender electric bass, and George DeHart on drums, augmented by Cal Green on guitar. Since recording the demo tape, Green and Ballard had tightened "The Twist" and slowed it down to a straight-eight shuffle that made the song more danceable. "Hank moved the song into E-natural," says Green, "and that allowed me to play open chords. That gave it a bigger sound. I was still playing Jimmy

Reed but now it sounded different, almost country." To get the
song moving, the band borrowed the opening, descending
three notes, beginning with the same rim shot, that they had
used on a 1956 Midnighters recording called "Tore Up Over
You." But whereas Green had played a T-Bone Walker-flavored
blues figure above the two saxophones on "Tore Up Over You,"
on "The Twist" he laid back and let the horns introduce the
song without him.

The distinctive saxophone solo on "The Twist" was provided by Ray Felder, a Cincinnati native who had played several
times on the prestigious Jazz at the Philharmonic tours before
settling down as one of King's steadiest session men. Whereas
the tenor saxist on the Florida demo of "The Twist" had gone off
on a honking solo that conflicted with the flow and rhythm of
the song, Felder effortlessly blended in so naturally on the studio version that, when the song was later covered in Philadelphia, "the saxophone player . . . played my solo almost note for
note," Felder said later.

Ballard had altered most of the lyrics, changed the song's
point of view, and softened its ambiguities. "Everybody is doin'
the Twist," he had sung on the demo version. "Everybody is
doin' the Twist; it's a crazy thing, goes like this." But to increase
the immediacy of the later recording he changed "The Twist"
from a third-person commentary to a direct invitation to the listener to get up and dance: "C'mon, baby, let's do the Twist."
Perhaps as an unconscious borrowing from Jelly Roll Morton's
"Winin' Boy Blues" or Buster Bennett's "I Want to Boogie Woogie," Ballard rewrote "You should see my baby do the Twist" in
the demo version to "You should see [pause] my little sis."
(Perhaps it wasn't unconscious: A year later, on a song called
"Look at Little Sis," he sang, "Hey hey hey hey, Mama, look at
Sis, she's out in the backyard shakin' like this!") Ballard also
toned down some of the demo's sexuality, particularly the
Midnighters's constant background chant of "up and down and
round and round"—suspicious imagery, to be sure—by making it
the more dancelike "round and around and around and around."

"The Twist" was the first of four numbers the Midnighters recorded that day, but it was not the song that Henry Glover, King Records's black in-house producer, was concentrating on as the group's next possible hit. That honor went to their second performance, a ballad called "Teardrops on Your Letter," written by Glover himself. And since Glover called the creative shots at King, he assigned his "Teardrops on Your Letter" as the A-side of the next single and consigned "The Twist" to be its B-side. The composer of "The Twist" was listed solely as Hank Ballard, even though the melody extended from the earlier song he'd cowritten with Cal Green (not to mention "What'cha Gonna Do?"). "I wasn't taking care of business," Green laments, with some bitterness. "I didn't go in and sign a contract as one of the writers. I was off somewhere with a woman or something." Brother Joseph Wallace also received no credit: "I'd accepted Jesus Christ as my savior and gospel music was my life, so I just let it go," he shrugged many years later.

"I'll Pray For You," which Ballard had hoped would be the flipside of "The Twist," was the third song recorded at the November 11 session, but neither it nor the day's final entry, "Everybody Does Wrong Sometime," was ever released as a single. They showed up on the group's next album, *The One & Only Hank Ballard and the Midnighters*.

As part of his new contract, Ballard's name was now emblazoned on the dark blue label—Hank Ballard and the Midnighters—of his debut King single when it came out in January 1959. "Teardrops on Your Letter," a moody, soulful number, turned out to be the group's biggest hit in four years, rising to number four on the rhythm and blues charts in April and even dipping briefly into pop's Hot 100. But at dances and hops, deejays turned it over to the uptempo side, and on April 6, 1959, "The Twist" entered *Billboard*'s R&B chart. The song remained in the running for ten weeks, topping out at number sixteen. But even after it dropped off the charts that summer, "The Twist" continued to simmer.

3: They're Really Twistin' on Bandstand!

"I may have started the nation Twisting, but I couldn't have
done it without Dick Clark and 'American Bandstand.'"
—Chubby Checker

"Syd Nathan, I loved the man, but he couldn't pick a hit to save
his soul," says Hank Ballard. "He hated 'The Twist.' But when
James Brown brought him 'Please, Please, Please,' he hated that
too. Said, 'What is this shit?' So what did he know?" Ballard
laughs at the memory. But Nathan, who didn't know a hit from
shinola, was nonetheless the owner — the publisher — of "The
Twist," for it was standard procedure that rhythm and blues
artists signed over the publishing rights of their songs to their
record companies. As Nathan had once told one of his promotion men, Dickie Kline, "The first thing you learn is everyone is
a liar, and the only thing that matters is the song. Buy the song,
own the song, but remember, no matter what anyone tells you,
they are liars until they have convinced you that they are telling
the truth." A song that you owned didn't lie. Both the song and
you were protected by the 1909 Copyright Act, backed by the
power of the U.S. government. Your song made you a few pen-
nies every time someone bought it on a record or a music sheet.
And if you were a member of Broadcast Music, Incorporated
(BMI), which Nathan was, there was a faceless army of people
out there who collected royalties for your song whenever it was
played on radio, on TV, and in public places. The music industry was a bunch of rat bastards who'd sell their sisters, but a
song — if it was the right song — would work tirelessly for you
like your own dear mother, bless her poor old heart.

Sydney Nathan was an unlikely man to be at the center of
"The Twist" phenomenon. Born in Cincinnati in 1904, he was,

14

in writer Peter Grendysa's words, a "tough Runyonesque record man . . . [who] was a myopic, anemic, asthmatic, overweight high-school dropout." He wore glasses with "Coke bottle" lenses and spoke in a gruff, gravelly voice he might have picked up from thirties' gangster movies. For a couple of years in the early forties, he owned a record shop that catered to the hillbillies whom the wartime factories had brought into Cincinnati from West Virginia, Kentucky, and Tennessee. By 1944, when a dispute between the American Federation of Musicians and the major record companies brought record production nearly to a standstill, Nathan decided to open his own operation. He took his "trust no one" philosophy to its logical conclusion by making King Records the most self-contained setup of any nonmajor record company; everything from studio recording to record pressing to the manufacture of record sleeves and shipping cartons to the actual shipment of records was done under the roof of one 9,000-square-foot factory building at the dead end of Brewster Avenue, where nothing escaped Nathan's owlish eyes. In a cartoon depiction of assembly line efficiency, the recording studio was located at one end of the building and the chute where the boxes of finished records came down was at the other. In between was a large room where fourteen presses could turn out 10,000 platters a day like so many pancakes.

King Records was, however, an independent label geared for the specialty markets of country and western and, later, rhythm and blues. Though an occasional King record, such as Lonnie Johnson's 1948 "Tomorrow Night," the Dominoes' 1951 "Sixty Minute Man," and Bill Doggett's 1956 "Honky Tonk," broke through to the pop charts, King lacked the connections to be a steady hitter in the big leagues. Compounding the problem was Syd Nathan's growing aversion to payola—"It's a dirty rotten mess," he told a Cincinnati reporter—which certainly didn't endear him to disc jockeys. For these and other reasons (perhaps the timing wasn't right), King Records did not have the resources, or at least did not sufficiently marshal those it had, to give "The Twist" the push it needed in 1959 to escape the rhythm and blues ghetto. But as any record man will tell you, there is such a thing as a "natural hit," and if people are allowed to hear it, they'll want to hear it again and again and again . . . until they gag on it.

Ralph Bass, who had produced Hank Ballard's earlier sessions, remembered the effect that "The Twist" had on southern audiences almost from the outset. "I remember in Atlanta, Georgia, when 'The Twist' came out," he told radio producer Jon Fox. "Hank Ballard was the featured act at this big club and they were lined . . . the whites were lined up, they were lined up, blacks and whites together, all down Auburn Avenue, to try to get into this club. The police came, man, and they said, 'We'll have a riot. Let 'em alone. Let 'em go.' So here, whites and blacks together."

"The Twist," Hank Ballard told writer Rick Coleman, "first broke out in Baltimore. We were at the Royal Theater for ten days. The kids over there caught on to it and took it to 'The Buddy Deane Show' [a popular TV dance party in Baltimore similar to Dick Clark's 'American Bandstand']." Apparently, the teenagers on "The Buddy Deane Show" had made up their own dance to "The Twist," and their improvised movements spread to West Philadelphia, where Clark's national ABC-TV show emanated from station WFIL at Forty-sixth and Market streets. Ballard continued: "[Deane] called Dick Clark and said, 'Man, you should see the kids over here. They're onto a record called "The Twist" by Hank Ballard and the Midnighters. They're dancin' and not even touchin'.'" In his book *Rock, Roll and Remember*, Dick Clark recalled it differently: "I saw a black couple doing a dance that consisted of revolving their hips in quick, half-circle jerks, so their pelvic regions were heaving in time to the music. The white kids around them watched, fascinated. Some started to imitate the dance." Clark said he told the cameramen to keep away from the couple because their moves were too suggestive for the show. "It looked like something a belly-dancer did to climax her performance." But he immediately went over and asked them, "What do you call that dance you were just doing?" They answered, "The Twist." By the following day, Clark noticed that half a dozen couples had "gotten the hang of it," and that the Twist was catching on.

Clark's recollections may be a little fuzzy, particularly because black kids were rarely if ever seen on "American Bandstand" in 1959-60. In a high-spirited 1993 film documentary by Canadian director Ron Mann called *Twist*, several of the former teenage regulars from "American Bandstand" sheepishly confessed to copying dances such as the Strand at black clubs and then tacitly being encouraged by the "American Bandstand" staff to execute the new steps on-air and claim them as their own inventions. According to "American Bandstand" dancer Jimmy Peatross, "We had to say we made it up." His former partner, Joan Buck Kiene, and fellow dancers Carole Scaldeferri Spada and Joe Fusco agreed. Dick Clark didn't want to hear about them picking up new dances from black kids in West Philly.

It is difficult to overestimate the effect that Richard Wagstaff Clark had on rock and roll music in the late 1950s. Clark himself was no youngster (he was born in Mount Vernon, New York, on November 30, 1929), but he had the clean-cut, boyish look of a high-school class president. After his local TV program, "Bandstand," went nationwide as "American Bandstand" on August 5, 1957, beaming out to 105 ABC network affiliates and some forty million viewers, Clark had the nation's teenagers twisted around his little finger. The post office delivered an average of 15,000 letters a week to Clark's cubbyhole offices. The Trendex Report, an early TV ratings survey, reported that "American Bandstand" was number one in its time period (3:00 to 4:30 P.M.), garnering "a 5.7 rating, with a 35.6 share of the audience— 62 percent higher than CBS and 35 percent greater than NBC." These impressive numbers gave Clark enormous control over the country's musical direction. "[W]hatever we played, everybody else had to play," Clark told record executive Joe Smith, "because a kid, say, in Keokuk would call a station and say, 'I heard it yesterday on "Bandstand." How come you're not playing it?'" A St. Louis record store owner told *Billboard* that

Clark's program was "the greatest stimulant to the record business we as dealers have ever known. Many dealers have installed TV sets in their record departments and extended teenagers an invitation to see the show in the stores."

Although Clark showcased rhythm and blues and rock and roll acts of all descriptions—after all, he had to fill ninety minutes every day Monday through Friday and another half hour on Saturdays—he found it more convenient to spotlight local talent (which was rarely rock-and-roll) and more profitable to appeal to the softer segment of his audience, the ones who bought most 45-RPM records: young girls, characterized by writer Greg Shaw as "the ones in the suburbs who wanted big fluffy candy-colored images of male niceness on which to focus their pubescent dreams." This pandering to adolescent feminine tastes, coupled with Clark's unprecedented power to turn a catchy record into a national sensation with only a few spins, brought about through unnatural selection what amounted to the degeneration of rock and roll into a safe, homogenized, easily digested curd, free of black or hillbilly regionalisms, performed either by wavy-haired, sparkling-toothed Adonises in white sweaters or polite, light-skinned young blacks dressed up like bible salesmen. As a good corporate employee, Clark was in the business of promoting marketable teen-idol product, not rock and rollers. Although ABC's network executives and "American Bandstand"'s sponsors would have housebroken the wild, indigenous, underclass music with or without Dick Clark, it is rock and roll's greatest irony that the man who presided over its gelding is today seen as its patron saint.

In May 1960, a new Hank Ballard and the Midnighters single, "Finger Poppin' Time," entered the Hot 100. Dick Clark aired it once or twice on "American Bandstand." For a couple of weeks the record hovered in the sixties, and then in mid-June it fell to number seventy-four. However, before "Finger Poppin' Time" could plummet into obscurity, Hank Ballard and the Midnighters rushed into Philadelphia on June 22, a Wednesday afternoon, to lip-synch and finger-snap along with the song in front of "American Bandstand"'s massive teen audience. This rescuscitation got the record rising again, and by mid-July it was leaping like Lazarus. "Finger Poppin' Time" spent most of August and early September in the Top Ten. Despite Ballard's seven busy years as an important rhythm and blues artist, "Finger Poppin' Time" was his first major pop hit, and he owed a great deal of its success to Dick Clark. But this success came at a cost, because during that time the concentrated media push behind "Finger Poppin' Time" assured that no other Hank Ballard and the Midnighters recording would get any attention until "Finger Poppin' Time" started fading.

Once again, Ballard's reluctance to let loose of a catchy tune had prompted him to create "Finger Poppin' Time" essentially as an extension of "The Twist." Spurred by the record's success and its rhythmic and melodic similarity to "The Twist," not to mention the Twist's continuing underground popularity as a dance, King Records reissued "The Twist" itself, and by mid-July 1960, the single made its way into *Billboard*'s Hot 100 for the first time. All it needed now was a friendly push from Dick Clark.

But, rather than spin Hank Ballard and the Midnighters' recording of "The Twist" on his show, Clark decided that the song needed to be redone, or as it was known in the business, "covered." Unlike a remake, a cover version was designed to capitalize on a recording that was currently popular or about to go on the charts. Because several major companies had made millions of dollars using covers to push aside and bury rhythm and blues platters on small labels during the early rock and roll years, the cover record had come to be seen as a symbol of racism and economic bullying. In this case, no major corporation was involved; one indie would simply be covering another's recording. But this small, independent company, Cameo-Parkway Records, possessed one major advantage. The rock and roll media's top power broker was setting up the deal. "I called Bernie Lowe at Cameo Records," Dick Clark wrote in his book. "I asked him if he remembered the record Hank Ballard had done a year or so ago called 'The Twist.' Bernie said he did." Clark then suggested, "It looks like it'll catch on. Why don't you turn the song upside down or sideways or whatever and do it again?" But Clark left more unsaid than said in his memoirs. "The Twist," by Hank Ballard and the Midnighters, was already out and cracking the charts and ready to break wide as soon as King Records and "American Bandstand" diverted their attention from "Finger Poppin' Time." Why record it again?

4: And It Goes Like This

"I love ya, you son-of-a-bitch. You made all
of my dreams come true."
—Chubby Checker, to Hank Ballard

Bernie Lowe founded Cameo Records in late 1956 and set up offices in the basement of his house in the Wincote area of North Philadelphia. (He later moved to 1405 Locust Street as his fortunes improved.) Born Bernard Lowenthal around 1918, Lowe was a Julliard-trained pianist playing, arranging, and conducting the orchestra on "The Paul Whiteman TV Teen Club" in the early fifties when he met Dick Clark, the announcer for the show's live Tootsie Roll commercials. The two became friends and, later, business associates.

Lowe's partner at Cameo was a Philadelphia-born (1917) comedy writer and lyricist named Kalman Cohen, who, in deference to another gag-man named Kal Cohen, dropped his surname and christened himself Kal Mann for the showbiz world. Mann and Lowe were old friends. Mann said recently that despite his later success as a hit songwriter, "My only musical training was one piano lesson that I took from Bernie Lowe after the war, and he said go home and play it. But I didn't have a piano." Though not a co-owner of Cameo Records, Mann was a major stockholder in the label and the owner of Cameo's publishing arm, Kalmann Music.

Lowe and Mann got into the record business as songwriters for Hill & Range Songs, a New York publishing company best known for its country music catalog. To present their songs, the two men made demo recordings on an old tape machine in Lowe's basement. Hearing a rumor that Hill & Range's hot new artist, Elvis Presley, collected teddy bears, they sat down and scribbled out a ditty for him called "(Let Me Be Your) Teddy Bear." The song clicked with Elvis right away. He recorded it at a January 1957 session for the soundtrack of his second film, *Loving You*. By then the tunesmiths had gone off on their own. "Our demos sounded better than the records that were getting made," Mann said, "and we thought maybe we should go into business for ourselves."

Their first releases on Cameo were singles by Arlene De Marco and the Quakertown Singers that were almost as old-fashioned as a cameo stone, but Lowe and Mann quickly realized that if they hoped to prosper in the modern music business they'd have to come to terms with the burgeoning new youth market. By the time Elvis was cuddling their "Teddy Bear" at the top of the charts late that summer, they had already written, produced, and released another Presley-style hit of their own. The artist was a local Sicilian-American singer-guitarist named Charlie Gracie (née Graci).

"Bernie was looking for an Elvis," Gracie said recently, "and he found me when I performed on Paul Whiteman's TV show. I was short and didn't look anything like Elvis, but I could play guitar better." Despite Gracie's prowess as a rambunctious rock-abilly, Lowe tamed him into a polite rocker whom even cranky parents could tolerate. Gracie's first Cameo release was "Butterfly," a four-chord song based on Guy Mitchell's 1956 number-one hit, "Singing the Blues." The song's most original line was its four-syllable hook, "you but-ter-fly," which, Kal Mann chuckled, "was 'My Dog Has Fleas' backward." When the record went to number one in April, it convinced Bernie Lowe that rock and roll—or at least an approximation of it—was the way to go, and convinced Kal Mann that the best way to write the next big hit was simply to rewrite somebody else's current hit. Over the next couple of years, Cameo would release a handful of credible records, including pickups they bought or leased from other producers—a late 1957 hit, "Silhouettes," by a black vocal group called the Rays being the most successful of these. As for Charlie Gracie, he was gone by early 1958. "I was expendable," Gracie said. "I was the first one to get screwed [by Cameo]. I sued for my royalties, settled for $40,000, and left."

Lowe and Mann launched Cameo's sister label, Parkway, in 1959 by letting Cameo sales director Jerry Fields put together "The Trial"—a so-called "break-in" record with a narrative broken up by snippets of popular songs. This strange genre, having originated with Bill Buchanan and Dickie Goodman's "Flying Saucer" records three years earlier, was stale by 1959, but "The Trial" at least announced Parkway's low expectations. Cameo-Parkway was, and would remain, largely a novelty operation characterized by Ruth Batchelor's "Lemon Drops, Lolly Pops and Double Bubble Gum" and then-TV actor Clint Eastwood's "Cowboy Wedding Song." Kal Mann could never quite shake his early wish to be a Tin Pan Alley comedy song-writer, and Bernie Lowe—whose "love of money exceeded his dislike of rock 'n' roll," according to British music writer Bill Millar—made no secret that his teenage daughter's tastes often guided the company's musical direction. "I never do anything, never put out a record, without letting her hear it first," Lowe once told Dick Clark. Writer Charlie Gillett described the Cameo-Parkway canon as "mostly crass stuff, impressive for its single-minded pursuit of the lowest common denominator, but generally lacking any originality which could be traced through to later records as any kind of 'influence.'" Jerry Gross, who sang tenor for one of Parkway's hitmakers, the Dovells of "Bristol Stomp" fame, was more succinct when he told writer Greg Milewski, "Cameo-Parkway was putting out crap. They were putting out garbage."

One important addition to Cameo-Parkway was Dave Appell, a Philadelphia guitarist with a feel for jazz. Born in Philadelphia in 1922, Appell had worked as an arranger for several big bands during his wartime service, including Jimmie Lunceford's legendary black orchestra. During the early fifties his Dave Appell Quartet was the studio band for comedian Ernie Kovacs's first TV program in Philadelphia. Changing the name of his group to the Applejacks, he recorded for Decca

Records and appeared prominently in the 1956 Alan Freed film, *Don't Knock the Rock*. A couple of years later, he and the Applejacks were playing in Las Vegas when they began to pine for their hometown.

"We got tired of being on the road," Appell said recently, "so we went back home to Philly and I started working for Cameo. First I did background vocals, then I became an engineer, played on sessions. I was a jack-of-all-trades." By 1958 he and the Applejacks broke into the national music charts with their Cameo recordings of "Mexican Hat Rock"—a jerky, jumped-up version of a familiar *huapango*, "Mexican Hat Dance"—followed by "Rocka-Conga," a rock and roll spoof of the conga line dance. In the summer of 1960, when Appell became the leader of Cameo-Parkway's house band, one of his first tasks was to record a new version of a rhythm and blues song by Hank Ballard and the Midnighters. A dance song called "The Twist."

Hank Ballard has two explanations as to why Dick Clark approached Cameo-Parkway instead of playing his original King Records single of "The Twist." In a fairly candid mood, he said, "Dick Clark didn't want to hear it because he thought it was just another one of my dirty songs!" He also believed that Syd Nathan and Dick Clark had cut a backroom deal—something along the line of: *Syd, I'll plug "Finger Poppin' Time" on "American Bandstand" if you license us "The Twist"!* "Dick started out playing my version of the song, then he switched to [Cameo's]," Ballard said. "Since Syd was the publisher of both versions, I know he sold me down the river." But during another interview, Ballard claimed more diplomatically that the Midnighters—always one of the chitlin circuit's most in-demand acts—were on a grueling tour of one-nighters in the South and couldn't make it into Philadelphia to promote the record, and so Clark opted for someone local. Joe Tarsia, who was Cameo-Parkway's electronics repairman at the time and later the company's sound engineer at Reco Arts Studio, said, "Dick had arranged for Hank to come on the show three times, and Hank stiffed him each time." Dave Appell recalled, "Hank Ballard's record was happening down South, but he wasn't a kid, and Dick Clark's show was for teenagers."

Clark himself has dodged the issue altogether, but in all likelihood all of these reasons contributed in some degree to his decision to find another "Twist." He was certainly wary of Ballard's rascally reputation. Ballard's "Sexy Ways" and the "Annie" trilogy had been widely banned several years earlier. Also, besides being a pure rhythm and blues outfit that made few concessions to white teenagers, the Midnighters were a raucous bunch, notorious for dropping their trousers onstage (revealing longjohns) and ravishing female groupies backstage. Clark wanted an artist with a more wholesome image, someone who wouldn't embarrass him and his sponsors. Letting Ballard and the guys promote "Finger Poppin' Time" on national television was one thing, but allowing them to represent a dance that Clark was certain could be an "American Bandstand" sensation was quite another. He saw a chance to promote "The Twist" into a hit record, and he wanted control over its presentation.

If "The Twist" had aroused his interest a year earlier, Dick Clark could have gone Syd Nathan at King Records one better and done the whole job himself, including hyping the record on national TV. In the heady final days of the late fifties, besides coproducing his own coast-to-coast program (through his Click Corporation and Drexel TV Productions), Clark shared in the ownership of the successful Jamie and Swan record labels, a few music publishing firms (including Sea-Lark Enterprises and January Music), a talent management company (SRO Artists), a record-pressing plant (Mallard Pressing Company—co-owned by Cameo's Bernie Lowe), and a full-service record distributorship (Chips Distribution, also co-owned by Lowe). He wouldn't have needed any help from the outside. But only a couple of months earlier, on May 2, 1960, Dick Clark had been dragged down to Washington, D.C., and publicly humiliated by the Oren Harris Subcommittee on Legislative Oversight in the U.S. House of Representatives concerning his sizable record industry holdings, as well as his publishing interests in over a dozen songs that he had spun into gold on "American Bandstand."

In the early months of this congressional investigation into commercial bribery—"payola"—in the music business, long before Clark was subpoenaed to appear, ABC had glimpsed what was coming. Leonard Goldenson, president of American Broadcasting Company, summoned Clark to his office in Manhattan and gave him an ultimatum: "Which would you like to be, in the music business or the television business?" Clark agreed to divest himself of his music holdings in order to stay on the air. (His business partner and TV producer, Tony Mamarella, chose to leave "American Bandstand," so Clark sold him his shares in several companies, including Swan Records.) Although Clark's decision saved him from being savaged during the subcommittee hearings, he remains bitter about it. "At the time, I was a fifty percent owner in Swan Records," he told Joe Smith. "And we used our own acts, which people looked at as a conflict of interest. I always find that amazing because I'm certain that Lawrence Welk, the biggest music publisher I knew, was using some of his copyrights on his show. But we got criticized for it."

One conflict of interest had been a $7,000 "royalty" that Bernie Lowe had paid to one of Clark's personal corporations for plugging Charlie Gracie's "Butterfly" on "American Bandstand." Clark, it turned out, had a great deal of stock in Cameo Records's hit single because Lowe had given him 25 percent of "Butterfly" 's publishing rights. The "composer" of the record's B-side, "Ninety-nine Ways," was one Anthony September, a pseudonym for Tony Mamarella, who made just as much off the single as did the composers of the A-side. Lowe also bestowed upon Clark half of the performance rights to a Stroll-friendly song called "Back to School Again" (recorded for Cameo by a forty-two-year-old black vaudevillian named Timmie "Oh Yeah" Rogers), which Clark then played regularly during a brief "American Bandstand" craze for the Stroll line dance.

"Dick Clark was really a silent partner at Cameo," Charlie Gracie opined many years later.

In light of the well-publicized payola hearings, the subcommittee's personal chastisement (one senator referred to Clark's extensive dealings as "Clarkola"), and the earlier ultimatum he had received from ABC, whatever arrangement Clark made with Bernie Lowe now, in 1960, had to be much more subtle than a royalty or a dividend. Perhaps more innocently, Clark simply demanded a crucial period of exclusivity wherein Cameo-Parkway's artist could perform "The Twist" only on "American Bandstand." As he later wrote in *Rock, Roll and Remember*, "The Twist broke as headline news. . . . Most of the country first saw it done on 'American Bandstand.' All anyone had to do was tune in between 3:30 and 5:00 to see it live from Philadelphia. The Twist was the rage and we had the patent on it."

Swan Records' top solo artist, Freddy Cannon, whom Clark had originally introduced on "American Bandstand" back when he owned half of Swan, recalls that he had the first crack at doing "The Twist." "There's been too much bullshit written about 'The Twist,' so I'm gonna tell ya the real story," says Cannon. "[Swan co-owner] Bernie Binnick and I drove down to Baltimore to do Buddy Deane's TV show, because 'American Bandstand' was blacked out in Baltimore and if you didn't do Buddy's show you didn't sell in Baltimore. Buddy primarily had black artists on his show, but he liked me. My new record, 'Way Down Yonder in New Orleans,' was just beginning to break. After I came off, Deane said, 'Bernie, watch the kids on this next record,' and he played 'The Twist' by Hank Ballard. The kids started going crazy. Bernie said, 'Gimme that record.' So he took it back up to Philadelphia with us. Next day I did 'Bandstand.' Bernie took the record into Dick's office and played it for him. I remember I was standing there by Dick's desk. Dick said, 'I can't play that, it's too black. Give it to Freddy here and we'll play it.' Bernie said, 'I can't do that. "Way Down Yonder in New Orleans" is breaking.'" As it turned out, Cannon would've had plenty of time to cover "The Twist," because the song wasn't recorded for another six months or so, and by then Cannon's career had gone into a slump. But in retrospect he says he's glad he didn't. "Anybody could've had a hit with 'The Twist,' but Hank Ballard is the only one who *should've* had a hit with it."

It's rumored that Danny and the Juniors—also on Swan Records at the time and managed by one of Bernie Lowe's former business partners, Artie Singer—likewise had an early shot at recording the song. According to engineer Joe Tarsia, "I had always heard that the [instrumental] tape for 'The Twist' was made for Danny and the Juniors." But Dave White, a member of the group and the cowriter of their big hit "At the Hop," recently said, "That's not true. Whoever started that story might've got it mixed up with 'Twistin' U.S.A.,' which was a hit for us *and* Chubby. We both used the same [instrumental] tracks."

Swan Records' office was right next door to Cameo, located in the same suite of offices on the sixth floor of a downtown Philadelphia office building, and the two companies, though separate entities, used some of the same musicians and producers. For example, the creative team of Bob Crewe and Frank Slay produced Freddy Cannon and, later, Danny and the Juniors for Swan, and the Silhouettes for Cameo. Whenever Clark visited one company, all he had to do was walk next door to see the other. In this case, whatever his earliest intentions, he ultimately turned to Bernie Lowe, who was currently supplying "American Bandstand" with a handsome, Sinatra-style teen idol named Bobby Rydell (née Ridarelli). Lowe also had on his roster a cherubic and polite young black artist named Ernest Evans.

Evans had been born nineteen years earlier, on October 3, 1941, in the South Carolina farming community of Spring Valley, but his parents, Raymond and Eartie, brought him to South Philadelphia when he was ten. His father's steady work in construction provided Ernest and his two younger brothers with a comfortable upbringing. "I sang in church," he told writer Wayne Jancik. "My whole life was around the church.

We were a Baptist kind of people." He attended the same school, South Philadelphia High, as teen faves Fabian and Frankie Avalon, and during his time there he sang lead with a doo-wop quartet called the Quantrells, roughly named after Quantrill's Raiders, a Confederate guerrilla outfit during the Civil War. His buddies in the group called him Fat Ernie. After graduation he worked in Henry Coltapiano's poultry shop on South Ninth Street, where he'd sing as he went about his chores. One of them was plucking and cutting chickens—a dull, unsavory job, but one the media would later fluff up into a demeaning shorthand characterization of him: ex-chicken plucker. Coltapiano, a balding man with a pencil mustache and an eye on show business, decided that anyone who could sing as happily as a lark while jerking feathers out of dead birds had to have *something*. He shortened his own name to Henry Colt, made himself the kid's manager, and introduced him to his friend Kal Mann at Cameo-Parkway.

Ernie had a pleasant and distinctive singing voice, but his specialty was imitating other artists. In time he would use his gift of mimicry to recreate a hit that was already on the charts. It would be the cover record to end all cover records, so faithful to the original that even the artist he copied, Hank Ballard, wasn't sure at first who was singing.

5: Twistin' Time Is Here

> "I've always liked physical action that approaches that of a religious revival. A going crazy is what I was looking for, where the music is so good you lose control. 'The Twist' did that."
> —Chubby Checker

In late 1959, according to Ernest Evans, "Dick Clark needed someone to do a singing card for his family. And the kind of Christmas card he was putting together involved [a recording of] the sounds of different artists of the day doing 'Jingle Bells.' He needed someone doing impressions. The word got back to him that I could do that sort of thing." Evans claimed that Bernie Lowe and Kal Mann already knew who he was. "I had gone to that record company like a hundred times. . . . They kept throwing me out! But I kept going back." Finally his persistence—and a good word from Henry Colt—paid off when Lowe asked him to record Clark's novelty song, mimicking Fats Domino and other popular rock and roll artists. Evans told Wayne Jancik: "Now, I was in the studio doing a Fats Domino bit at the piano. I was rehearsing and was so excited about my chance. . . . Dick Clark's wife Barbara comes in. She says, 'You're Chubby.' I'm chubby, yeah. 'You're Chubby Checker, like Fats Domino, 'cause you're doing one of his songs.' After she said that, the company got interested in me."

When the Clarks sent the record out to all their friends and business acquaintances for the holidays, it got an enthusiastic response. "Then they wanted me to do something like this 'Jingle Bells' thing. And 'The Class,' my first record, was a clone of that." For "The Class," Bernie Lowe or Kal Mann changed the song from "Jingle Bells" to "Mary Had a Little Lamb." Backed by a swinging little band, Evans was the teacher asking several of his pupils to sing a verse. Along with Fats Domino, there were the Coasters chanting with a "Charlie Brown" staccato rhythm; Elvis singing to the tune of "Hound Dog" ("You ain't nuthin' but a little lamb"); drummer Cozy Cole, of "Topsy, Part 2" fame, pounding out a cowbell solo as he bellowed "Mary, Part Two"; and the Chipmunks, using the sped-up voices of both Evans and Bobby Rydell. "The Class" came out in spring of 1959 as Parkway Records's fifth single; the name on the label was Chubby Checker. "I didn't like it," he admitted later. "But there were no Chubby Checkers around. It was kind of unique."

(This was not the first time a rhythm and blues Domino became a Checker. Bill Brown, the deep-toned bass vocalist of the group the Dominoes, became so popular after he sang lead on the million-selling "Sixty Minute Man" that he left the Dominoes in 1952 and formed his own group, the Checkers.)

After Chubby Checker lip-synched "The Class" on "American Bandstand" at the end of April, the single sold briskly enough to reach number thirty-eight on the pop charts. His next three Parkway releases carried on the cuteness with "The Jet" / "Ray Charles-ton," "Sampson and Delilah" / "Whole Lotta Laffin'," and "Dancing Dinosaur" / "Those Private Eyes Keep Watching Me," but none of them made the slightest ripple. "The Jet," a corny mishmash of melodies marred by squeaky outer-space sound effects, hinted at things to come because it was an attempt to create a new dance, though what the Jet was supposed to look like on the dance floor was never made clear. Chubby Checker seemed to be on a slope back to oblivion, a modest one-hit wonder.

On the heels of "Dancing Dinosaur," though, came Chubby Checker's carbon-copy rendering of "The Twist" (Parkway 811). Talking with record executive Joe Smith, Checker recalled: "In 1959 [sic] Kal Mann called me from Cameo and said, 'We got this record called "The Twist." '

"I said, 'Hank Ballard and the Midnighters did that tune.'

"Kal said, 'Yes, I know, but I think we can put a little dance to it, and then you can show people how it's done.'

"I said okay."

The basic tracks for "The Twist" were probably recorded around June or early July 1960, in Cameo's sixth-floor offices at 1405 Locust Street, near Broad Street, across from Philadelphia's Academy of Music. "The company office had three or four rooms," Dave Appell recalled, "and we'd converted one of them into a fourteen-by-nineteen-foot studio. It was off to the left as you walked in the front door of the office. We put a carpet on the floor and rugs on the walls to dampen the sound. We had a mono Ampex machine with four inputs and a [mixing] board worth about ten dollars. That's where we cut our basic tracks—our instrumental tracks. We'd always have to wait until after six o'clock in the evening. After we'd finish recording we'd take the tape to Reco Arts Studio [at 212 North Twelfth Street], over by Market, and overdub the vocals there, mono to mono. 'The Twist' was one of the first dates I did [as bandleader] for Cameo."

As Dick Clark described the makeshift studio, "If they wanted echo they had to wait until everyone in the building went home, then they'd run a set of speakers down the hall and stick them in the john with a microphone. The studio itself was about twenty-five feet square. In one corner was a partitioned-off control room made of plywood with a little window cut in it so they could see out into the rest of the studio. In one corner of the control room was an Ampex quarter-inch tape recorder on rollers." Joe Wissert, a Cameo employee, remembered the first time somebody showed the studio to him after "The Twist" became a hit. "God, I couldn't believe it was cut in this little room. Because of the booth, the studio was angular, and I coudn't imagine how they managed to get all the instruments in there at the same time without stepping on top of each other. And the console was this tiny Ampex with a green face and rotary knobs."

Appell called in several musicians to record "The Twist."

Leroy Lovett, the pianist, was the only black sideman on the session. Drummer Ellis Tollin and saxophonist Buddy Savitt were white. And so was the bass player. "He was a milk man, I forget his name. I'd never worked with him before and never worked with him after that session," Appell said. This hastily assembled group sat down, listened to Hank Ballard and the Midnighters's record together on a small phonograph, then lifted almost note-for-note Henry Glover's King Records studio band's arrangement. "We gave it a cymbal beat, with a straight-eight feel that wasn't on Hank's record," he said.

When the instrumental track — recorded live — was finished, Appell put together the final session a few days or perhaps a week later at Reco Arts Studio, where engineer Emil Corson added his expertise to the mix. The Dreamlovers — a black Philadelphia vocal group that would later record the doo-wop hit "When We Get Married" for another label — stood in for the Midnighters. And Checker, for his part, did a stunning job imitating Ballard's squealy baritone. "At Reco we recorded Chubby and the Dreamlovers together," said Appell. "They sang along in the studio with our instrumental track onto another mono machine, and that was it." Checker said it took him only thirty-five minutes to record three vocal takes of "The Twist." Kal Mann recalled that Chubby's only problem was going flat on the word "sleepin' " on the second chorus: "Daddy is sleepin' and Mama ain't around; Daddy's just *sleep-in'* and Mama ain't around." "If you listen closely to the record, you can hear we never did get it right," said Mann.

A couple of weeks after Parkway released the single, Dick Clark gave Checker and the Twist a deluxe introduction. Rather than book him on "American Bandstand," where he had already begun playing "The Twist," Clark decided the best showcase for the singer was his popular "The Dick Clark Show," which had been broadcasting every Saturday from the Little Theater at 240 West Forty-fourth Street in Manhattan since early 1958. This weekend TV program differed in a couple of important ways from the weekday "American Bandstand." First, it aired in the evening from 7:30 to 8:00 P.M., leading directly into television's coveted "prime time," when most people—including Mom and Dad—were plopped down in front of their black-and-white TV sets. Secondly, the showcase was a theater, not a dance floor, where nearly five hundred studio kids sat watching a stage show that included production numbers.

On Saturday, August 6, 1960, Clark was addressing his biggest weekly audience when the curtains parted and he brought out Chubby Checker, dressed nicely in black slacks and a checkered sportscoat, not only to lip-synch along with "The Twist," but also to give America its first Twist lessons. "Just pretend you're wiping your bottom with a towel as you get out of the shower and putting out a cigarette with both feet," intoned Chubby, who indeed was chubby during his first appearance, before all those Twist lessons sweated a few pounds off him. Chubby or his choreographer had masterfully toned down the Twist enough that he was able to swivel his hips—a breakthrough for television—without seeming obscene about it. More important, the Twist that Chubby demonstrated that August night on "The Dick Clark Show" was simplicity itself, so elemental in its execution that anybody, no matter how awkward or uncoordinated, could finesse his or her way through it. The Twist was probably the world's easiest dance. And that, as Checker was quick to point out, was precisely why it was such a great dance for everyone. "More skilled dancers add their own interpretation to the basic Twist steps and for them it takes on additional interest and more intricate variations," he would later tell *Ebony* magazine. "There's something in the Twist to appeal to all age groups."

In the months to come, the media had a field day taking swipes at the Twist merely by describing how it was done. "The dance is simple: The feet move slightly while everything else Twists," said *Newsweek*, which termed the Twist a "sacroili-act." *Time* magazine was just as colorful: "The dancers scarcely ever touch each other or move their feet. Everything else, however, moves. The upper body sways forward and backward and the hips and shoulders twirl erotically, while the arms thrust in, out, up and down with the piston-like motions of a baffled bird keeper fighting off a flock of attacking blue jays." Comedian Bob Hope likened the Twist to "a dog coming out of water."

Hank Ballard has said often that he wrote "The Twist" after watching the Midnighters improvise the familiar dance step, throwing up one leg and then the other, but Cal Green remembered it differently: "We had a dance routine for all our songs on stage, but when we did the Twist it was just a wiggle." Green, a small man with a thin, well-disciplined body, demonstrated the Midnighters' moves, keeping both feet together and wiggling only his hips and upper legs in a movement reminiscent of the original twist from the Mess Around and Ballin' the Jack. "All that other stuff came later with Chubby," Green said. Checker himself explained, "Well, I'd seen [Ballard] perform it. But he didn't do the Twist. Ever seen in the old movies where the Indians catch the settlers and then they dance around them? Well, that's what Hank Ballard would do to the song on stage. But, you know, there were kids in the ghetto doing a Twist thing and a little slipped in to 'Bandstand'; it was some other tune. And it inspired me and when my 'Twist' came out we decided that the Twist would be like putting out a cigarette with both feet, or like coming out of the shower and wiping your butt with a towel." He claimed that he had originally introduced the Twist earlier in the summer at the Rainbow Club in Wildwood, New Jersey, and that by night's end he'd gotten the whole place up on the dance floor, Twisting.

Where this basic movement of the Twist—toweling one butt while grinding out another—came from is anybody's guess. Chubby confessed, "I truly don't know who came up with it!" But an early approximation of the Twist can be seen in a 1930 British film called *Cavalcade*, a musical comedy about music-hall artists before World War I. In one scene a song-and-dance man, holding his elbows out and his fists at chest level and throwing his hips wildly to each side, demonstrated the Twist's basic movement as a comic turn-around gimmick at the edge of the stage. (The rotation on the balls of the feet might have come from military pivotal movements, such as about-face, left-face, and so on.) More recently, in the 1957 film *Jailhouse Rock*, Elvis Presley, whose shaking hips had been kept out of camera range during his final "Ed Sullivan Show" appearance earlier in the year, performed a primitive Twist in a poolside scene while singing "(You're So Square) Baby, I Don't Care." Such a simple (some say simple-minded) movement as the Twist could hardly have been "invented" as late as 1960.

The tamed-down Twist that Chubby Checker demonstrated for America was hardly the Twist that black kids in Baltimore had been dancing several months earlier. Though Freddy Cannon recalled from his afternoon on "The Buddy Deane Show" in late 1959 that the basic steps had been similar, the kids' movements were more fluid, more erotic, with more grind in the groin and more shimmy in the shoulders. Their Twist had evolved from the same early dance as had rock and roll's Jitterbug a few years earlier, and its origins were most likely improvised at the Savoy Ballroom, a hallowed Harlem dance hall that took up the second floor of an entire block of Lenox Avenue between 141st and 142nd streets.

In the late 1920s, the Savoy was the center of "swing," a hopped-up, supple jazz played by full bands. There were two bandstands at the Savoy; as one band went off, another one was already starting up the beat in order to keep the music going for the energetic, sneaker-shod male and female dancers who packed the ballroom's massive polished-wood floor. On Saturday nights the Savoy held "cutting contests"—a jazz term taken from jousting matches between rival musicians in so-called "battles of the bands"—and awarded prizes to the most creative participants. (These dance competitions were a holdover from antebellum America's cakewalks.) The northeast corner of the Savoy, called the Cats' Corner, was reserved for the best dancers. In time an acrobatic dance form evolved that allowed these youngsters a way to show their stuff, wow the bystanders, get some respect, and win a few dollars or some clothes from a local haberdashery. The dance was composed of a syncopated two-step, with the partners jumping and gyrating together while holding hands, and a "breakaway" in which they separated and went into their own improvisations, much like jazz soloists going off on their own riffs. The trick for the partners was to slip off into the breakaway and later return to each other without ever missing the beat. In 1928, when whites discovered this dance and took it downtown, they named it after Charles Lindbergh, the aviator who'd flown solo across the Atlantic Ocean without missing a beat the year before. The dance became known as the Lindy, or the Lindy Hop.

Listen to Malcolm X's description of doing the Lindy at a Boston club in the late thirties:

> As always, the crowd clapped and shouted in time with the blasting band. 'Go, Red, go!' Partly it was my reputation, and partly Laura's ballet style of dancing that helped to turn the spotlight—and the crowd's attention—to us. They never had seen the feather-lightness that she gave to lindy-ing, a completely fresh style—and they were connoisseurs of style. I turned up the steam, Laura's feet were flying; I had her in the air, down, sideways, around; backwards, up again, down, whirling. . . . A new favorite was being discovered; there was a wall of noise around us. I felt her weakening, she was lindying like a fighter out on her feet, and we stumbled off to the sidelines.

Vintage Lindy Hop dancing exists on film today thanks to a black improvisational group called Whitey's Savoy Lindy Hoppers, led by a Savoy Ballroom hoofer named Herbert White. After honing their skills in the Cats' Corner, White's half-dozen dancers went on the road and took the Lindy Hop halfway around the world. Fortunately for posterity, they happened to be in Hollywood in 1937, and anyone who wants to see the Twist's ancestor can watch Whitey's Savoy Lindy Hoppers go through their spirited leaps, air dances, and wacky footwork in the Marx Brothers classic *A Day at the Races*.

But the Lindy in its full glory remained a segregated dance. The white folks in downtown Manhattan picked up only the two-step and ignored the breakaway. By 1936 this simpler, less acrobatic Lindy had become a national dance craze called the Jitterbug after white bands appropriated swing music from Fletcher Henderson and the other black bandleaders who had more or less invented it. Newspapers reported with shock that teenagers were "jitterbugging in the aisles" at Benny "King of Swing" Goodman's Carnegie Hall concert that year. Two decades later the Jitterbug got hot again when rhythm and blues mutated into rock and roll. But the Lindy breakaway remained forgotten—until a clique of black teenagers in Baltimore brought it back in the late 1950s. "In a development as revolutionary as the first closed-couple waltz, the breakaway of the Lindy broke away to become a dance all by itself," wrote dance historian Gerald Jonas. And then in traditional fashion, white teenagers, white entertainers, and white businessmen were there to steal it (or at least a simplified form of it) and mis-name it "the twist" after another black pelvic dance movement entirely, the Mess Around. "African-derived improvisation had triumphed over European-style touch dancing," concluded Jonas.

But before it resurfaced in the Twist, a simplified break-away had showed up in late 1957 on, of all places, "American Bandstand," under the name the Bop. Anyone who claims that the Twist was the first modern rock and roll dance in which the partners stood apart and shook and wriggled at each other wasn't keeping up with rock and roll that year. The Bop apparently began within southern California's distinctive hot-rod culture, an amalgam of white hipsters and Chicano *vatos* and *pachucos* who had been grooving to the manic rhythm and blues of mad-raving honking tenor saxophonists like Big Jay McNeely and Wild Bill Moore since the late forties. Philadelphia's Bandstanders picked up the Bop when a couple of Los Angeles dancers were invited in as out-of-town guests on the program. The Bop was a strenuous workout: the partners, without touching, faced each other and jumped up and down in place to the beat of Gene Vincent's "Be-Bop-a-Lula," "Bluejean

Bop," and "Dance to the Bop," grinding their heels left and right when they landed.

Instantly popular on the show, the Bop inspired a couple of young Philadelphia songwriters named John Medora and David White to write a song called "Do the Bop." "We saw the kids doing it on 'Bandstand,' " Dave White recalled. "It was a strange dance. You hopped and kicked your right foot out and brought your heel down on the floor." John Medora remembered it as "a combination of the [later] Stomp and the Mashed Potatoes." When their producer, Artie Singer, took a demo of Medora singing "Do the Bop" to Dick Clark to get his opinion, Clark told them that the Bop wasn't going to last much longer, so maybe they should retitle it. David White's vocal group, Danny and the Juniors, duly rerecorded the song, with new lyrics, as "At the Hop" and Danny Rapp's voice replacing Medora's over the instrumental track. Half the song's publishing went to Dick Clark's January Music Company. "At the Hop," bolstered by the group's appearances on "American Bandstand," went to number one for five weeks in early 1958. "At the Hop" had a good beat, and you could Bop to it. The Bop was still fairly popular when Hank Ballard and the Midnighters began fooling around with "The Twist."

(Apparently this "commissioning" of a record for a new dance was common backstage at "Bandstand central." Clark himself said that if a new dance came along without a record to do it with, "I immediately called to tell my friends in the record business." For instance, when a line dance called the Stroll became popular on the show, Clark mentioned it to Nat Goodman, the manager of a white quartet called the Diamonds. "And I asked Nat, 'If we could have another Stroll-type record, you'd have yourself an automatic hit,' " Clark told Joe Smith. Goodman came back a week later with a song called "The Stroll." "We stick it on the air and it's a smash!" said Clark. The same thing happened when the Chalypso—a cross between the cha-cha and calypso—got hot on the program. Clark "commissioned" a guy to write a calypso-rhythmed song called "Lucky Ladybug" for Swan Records artists Billie and Lillie. The practice had become almost standard procedure by the time the Twist came along.)

Between the Midnighters' recording of "The Twist" demo in Miami in the spring of 1958 and the final master in November, another peculiarly American pastime had materialized long enough to limber up the nation's more daring adventurers for the hip-grinding movements of the Twist dance. In March, Arthur Melin and Richard Knerr, two entrepreneurs in their early thirties, were attending a toy fair in New York City. Melin and Knerr owned the Wham-O Manufacturing Company in San Gabriel, California, which only a year earlier had introduced to the toy world a plastic, aerodynamic plate called the "Frisbee." Now they were looking for another simple but million-dollar idea. An acquaintance at the fair told them about a bamboo hoop that Australian children exercised with in gym classes — possibly something they'd picked up from the Aborigines. The trick, said the friend, was to undulate your body in such a way as to keep the hoop spinning centrifugally around your torso and legs without letting it fall to the ground. When Melin and Knerr returned to southern California (home of the Bop), they made several bamboo hoops and let neighborhood children try them out. Soon the inventors switched over to the more malleable, lollipop-colored, high-density polyethylene plastic they used to make their Frisbees and fashioned it into long tubes that could then be bent into circles. By May their new hoop, three feet in diameter, went on sale for $1.98. Moving its origins from down under to the exotic city of Hilo, Hawaii, home of the hula dance, Melin and Knerr called their toy the Hula-Hoop.

Whether they realized it or not, the Hawaiian connection would sell the idea of hip-swiveling to white Americans as no amount of Messin' Around or Ballin' the Jack ever could. If Melin and Knerr had called their product the Swahili Hoop or the Congo Hoop, the white buying public probably would have rejected it outright. To them, anything associated with black culture was tinged with sin, a loss of inhibitions, a slide into the primitive. Hadn't white southern preachers already been screaming and railing about the "nigger rock 'n' roll bop," or, more politely, the "degenerate Negro music"? On the other hand, linking the plastic hoop to the semi-religious hula dance got around this marketing problem altogether. Although missionaries had originally tried to ban the hula, calling it "a very great and public evil" when they arrived in Hawaii in 1820, Americans after World War II considered the dance an innocent, if sensual and exotic Polynesian entertainment, and only the most prudish would denounce it.

The "game" of keeping the hoop moving around the body by swaying the hips caught on immediately with kids and, soon after, with their parents. Since Wham-O could only patent the name Hula-Hoop and not the hoop itself, other manufacturers spun off their own versions with such names as Spin-a-Hoop. Cheap ones cost as little as seventy-nine cents. A giant model, six feet in diameter and advertised as fun at cocktail parties for couples and moresomes, sold for $4.95.

By September a Hula-Hoop craze had hips grinding and asses swinging all over the country. According to the *New York Times*, Americans had already bought somewhere in the neighborhood of twenty million hoops of all sizes and colors for about $30 million. Wham-O sold over two million alone. Along with the hoop came the hoopla, as newspapers reported on Hula-Hoop marathons — Terri Seskin, age ten, of New York twirled a hoop around her midriff 4,010 times in forty-five minutes; James McDonald, age nine, of Chicago kept a hoop spinning over 21,000 times in three and a half hours. There were also the inevitable reports of damage to sacroiliacs and other rusty bones — Mrs. Dana Cramer, fifty-eight, fractured a hip in Akron, and Harold Dukes, twenty-five, of Michigan dislocated a vertebra.

As usually happens during a frivolous media whirl, record producers rushed into studios to contrive novelties such as

"Hoopa Hoola" by "Tonight Show" regular Betty Johnson and "Hula Hoop" by former "Tonight Show" host Steve Allen. The most popular was "The Hula Hoop Song," written by novice songwriters Donna Kohler and Carl Maduri, and recorded by both "Her Nibs" Miss Georgia Gibbs and bubbly-voiced Teresa Brewer. Gibbs was already famous for her 1955 number-one record, "Dance with Me, Henry," the most successful answer to Hank Ballard's "Work with Me, Annie." By 1958, her career waning, Georgia Gibbs had found herself on the Mafia-connected Roulette Records label, later to figure prominently in the marketing of the Twist dance. After she recorded "The Hula Hoop Song" on Friday, September 5, Gibbs warmed up the public by performing it that Sunday night on "The Ed Sullivan Show." Deejays and distributors had copies of "The Hula Hoop Song" in hand by Monday, and a day or two later she lip-synched the record on "American Bandstand." But Gibbs, approaching middle age, lacked the swinging hips or the hip swing to really put the song over, and besides, the hoop was wobbling and dropping fast. The Hula-Hoop had been a summer diversion; Johnson's "Hoopa Hoola" and the Gibbs and Brewer singles didn't enter the Hot 100 until autumn, when kids were going back to school. Her Nibs's recording, which only nibbled at *Billboard*'s Top Forty, was the most popular. By early November the records and the Hula-Hoop were gone. But the nation's temporary insanity had done its dirty work. The undulating genie had been unbottled.

6: Take Me by My Little Hand

"People started to talk about this dance because it was suggestive, it was nasty, it was dirty, it was sacrilegious, it was rebellious, it was as shocking as the first bikini."
—Chubby Checker, to British radio producer Louise Bruce

Hank Ballard recalled that he was floating half-asleep in a swimming pool on a bright azure day in Hallandale, Florida, a few miles north of Miami, listening to a pop station on a tinny little transistor radio when he first heard Chubby Checker's "The Twist." The record startled him fully awake. "At first I thought it was me," he said. "Hell, it sounded like me! I wondered what a big station was doing playing my record. But then I couldn't hear any drive in the voice, and the tracks were weak." Cal Green, cooling his heels in his hometown of Houston, Texas, serving a two-year stretch in the county jail for marijuana possession, had a similar reaction: "I thought it was us!" And why shouldn't they? "The Twist" by Hank Ballard and the Midnighters had been reissued a few weeks earlier and was already climbing up the charts. And this new recording sounded almost exactly like it.

Chubby Checker's single entered *Billboard*'s Hot 100 on the first of August at number forty-nine. (Ballard's original, enjoying its third week in the charts, sat four slots away at number fifty-three.) Checker leapt into the Top Forty following his demonstration of the Twist on "The Dick Clark Show." After being held off by Elvis Presley's "It's Now or Never" for a couple of weeks, "The Twist" finally slipped into the top position on September 19. (It also reached number one on the *Cash Box* pop chart.) That same week, Ballard's version of "The Twist," taking advantage of consumer confusion and riding the wake of

"Finger Poppin' Time," topped out at number twenty-eight. At the end of the month, Chubby donned a checkered jacket and officially accepted his gold record from Dick Clark on "American Bandstand" in front of the nation's Twist-happy teenagers.

Ballard's live studio cut was much looser and more swinging than the Parkway copy, but from a merchandising point of view, recasting "The Twist" in Chubby Checker's image was a stroke of genius. Hank Ballard was sleek and dark, with processed hair and cool, wary eyes. He was almost twenty-five, but older than his years. Having lived by his wits in both the Jim Crow South and the northern ghetto, he had few illusions about where he stood in American society. Behind his infectious laugh lurked an understandable resentment. Chubby Checker, on the other hand, was a big (five-foot-eleven), gregarious, light-skinned, expressive, working-class kid not yet out of his teens, as cuddly and telegenic as a teddy bear despite an elongated chin that dominated his face. As Dick Clark described him, "He was young, good looking, and a born ham whose hip-wiggling version of the dance often looked like a tricky exercise." In short, Chubby was, at least on the surface, a technicolor version of Freddy Cannon, Frankie Avalon, Fabian, and all the rest of the bland scream bait Dick Clark exhibited on "American Bandstand," except that he lacked their sex appeal. Checker seemed more like the class clown than the class Romeo. Why, parents could almost trust him with their daughters. And if any danger lingered about the Twist's ghetto origins, Dick Clark cannily dispelled it by inviting slapstick comic Jerry Lewis onto "American Bandstand" to give it a try under the tutelage of singer JoAnn Campbell. The spectacle of Jerry Lewis mugging ("Whaaaaa!") and twitching around the WFIL studios was enough to reduce the Twist to just another idiot diversion.

Some people, including Chubby Checker, have suggested that "The Twist" was actually the B-side of his record, and that "Toot," a novelty knockoff of the Royal Teens' 1958 hit "Short Shorts," was the intended top side. Recording engineer Joe

Tarsia said, "Keep in mind that Kal and Bernie were writers and they wanted to push their own songs first. 'The Twist' had low priority until Dick Clark wanted it." Checker himself recalled, "['Toot'] should have been the hit. But there was this guy in Pittsburgh named Porky Chedwick. He was on WEAM, or something [actually WAMO]. He said, 'I don't give a damn about no "Toot." I'm doing "The Twist".' . . . And 'The Twist' took off right there in that town." However, an early Parkway pressing of "The Twist" labels it as 811-A and "Toot" as 811-B. Also, in an industry in which an artist's new releases were generally spaced at least six weeks apart, "The Twist" came out immediately (perhaps within a few days or a week) after "Dancing Dinosaur" (810), suggesting that something compelled Parkway to hurry "The Twist" out the door and simultaneously kill "Dancing Dinosaur" (which today is so rare that many record collectors doubt it was ever released). What could be more compelling than a suggestion from Dick Clark himself to stop the presses on one record and rush out "The Twist" instead? It's doubtful that Clark would have clamored for a blatantly derivative piece of nonsense like "Toot." In the era before the modern music conglomerates dictated what the public had to listen to, dozens of rock and roll classics—from "Sh-Boom" and "Rock Around the Clock" to "Tequila" and "In the Still of the Nite"(not to mention Hank Ballard's "The Twist")—began as B-sides and were then flipped over by street-level disc jockeys. Chubby Checker's "The Twist" was almost certainly not one of them.

At some point after Checker's cover version became a hit, King Records went back into the studio and tampered with the Hank Ballard original to make it more marketable — and more like the Parkway recording. One element that Checker's "Twist" had that Ballard's didn't was Buddy Savitt's tenor sax grinding in the background during the verses. Since Parkway had copied King, turnabout was fair play; one of Syd Nathan's producers overdubbed a low but annoyingly grating saxophone growl into the background of Ballard's recording to match Checker's, and issued this doctored version under the same 1959 release number, King 5171. The label details remained the same, except that the type size of the title and group name were fattened on the reissue and Hank Ballard's name was made larger in an area just to the right of the donut hole. The recording number scratched into the deadwax of the original record was F-45-1308-1; on the reissue it was K-45-1308-X2. The "F" designation—engraved also into the deadwax of "Teardrops on Your Letter" on both the original and the reissue—denotes Federal Records, the King subsidiary for which Hank Ballard and the Midnighters were still working when the session was cut. The "K" on the later issue denotes King. Unfortunately, this inferior, overdubbed version of "The Twist" would appear on Hank Ballard's subsequent King albums, including *Singin' and Swingin'* and *24 Hits By Hank Ballard & His Midnighters*, and today it is probably the more familiar of the two.

This tampering with an existing recording was a common practice at King Records. Whenever a popular artist rerecorded one of the label's old hits, such as when LaVern Baker reinterpreted Lonnie Johnson's 1948 recording of "Tomorrow Night" or the Untouchables remade the Dominoes' 1951 hit "Sixty Minute Man," King pulled their original recordings out of the vaults, dusted them off, overdubbed them with "modern" choruses, and reissued the sweetened versions. Why should "The Twist" be any different? Syd Nathan was not the sort of guy to miss grabbing an extra dollar.

When Hank Ballard (left) first brought "The Twist" to Sid Nathan (right), president of King Records, Nathan didn't like the song. Photo courtesy of Alan Clark Archives.

Dick Clark (at top), on the lookout for offensive hip movements, monitors Jitterbugging couples on his Philadelphia-based "Bandstand" TV show in early 1957, several months before the show went national as "American Bandstand."

TV host Dick Clark (right) reportedly wanted rock and roll singer Freddy Cannon (left) to record a cover version of Hank Ballard's "The Twist." When Cannon declined the offer, Clark turned to his second choice, Chubby Checker.

Chubby Checker kicks the Twist into overdrive in *Twist Around the Clock*.

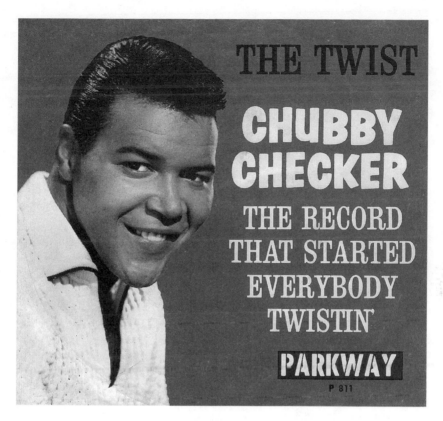

Parkway Records reissued Chubby Checker's "The Twist" with a picture
sleeve (above) in late 1961. The single became a number-one hit for the
second time.

The Peppermint Lounge on Manhattan's West Forty-fifth Street became the international mecca of the Twist in late 1961, after high society dropped in to dance.

Joey Dee (right), accompanied by chanting Starliters Larry Vernicri and Dave Brigati, sings "Peppermint Twist" in the film *Hey, Let's Twist!*.

The Dovells, featuring Len Barry (center), recorded the hit single "Bristol Twistin' Annie" and appeared in the film *Don't Knock the Twist*.

Sam Cooke, shown here in 1957, wrote and recorded one of the Twist oeuvre's few evergreen songs, "Twistin' the Night Away," in early 1962.

Fashion-show dancers Stephen Preston and Georgine Darcy Twist demurely to the live music of the Carrol Brothers in the film *Don't Knock the Twist*.

Film producer Sam Katzman (left) gives Chubby Checker a few pointers on how to create cinematic magic.

THE EXCITING MOVIE ABOUT THE SENSATION!

"HEY, LET'S TWIST!"

Out of New York's famed PEPPERMINT LOUNGE—
The Temple of the Twist!

PEPPERMINT Lounge

WITH THE STARS AND MUSIC THAT STARTED IT...FILMED WHERE IT HAPPENS EVERY NIGHT---THE STORY, THE SENSATION THAT'S SWEEPING THE NATION--INTO THE HEARTS OF YOUNG AND OLD!

Hey!
Joey Dee's
"HEY, LET'S TWIST"
record album is ready now—featuring
"HEY, LET'S TWIST"
"ROLY POLY"
"MOTHER GOOSE TWIST"
"I WANNA TWIST"

STARRING
JOEY DEE and THE STARLITERS · JO-ANN CAMPBELL · TEDDY RANDAZZO · KAY ARMEN · ZOHRA LAMPERT · DINO di LUCA

THE PEPPERMINT LOUNGERS · Produced by HARRY ROMM · Directed by GREG GARRISON · Original Screenplay by HAL HACKADY · A PARAMOUNT RELEASE

On the set of *Don't Knock the Twist*, actors Chubby Checker and Lang Jeffries discuss the merits of Stanislavsky's "Method" as it pertains to toweling one's backside.

Twisters grind and swivel to the rhythm of Louis Prima's band, the Witnesses, featuring honking tenor saxman Sam Butera, in *Twist All Night*.

7: Let's Twist Again, Like We Did Last Summer

"John, Jackie and the baby, too, if they can do it, so can you."
–Freddy King and Lula Reed, "Do the President Twist"

After "The Twist" died down at the end of 1960, Chubby Checker kept the dance on a slow burn. Following a number-one hit in early 1961 with "Pony Time" — a cover of Don Covay & the Goodtimers' original single that effectively killed it — Checker Twisted back into the Top Ten with an exciting sequel, "Let's Twist Again," which Kal Mann bragged he wrote in five minutes. " 'The Twist' was a twelve-bars blues," he said, "but I wrote 'Let's Twist Again' as a Tin Pan Alley song. I wanted it to be completely different." In any event, it was a well-crafted piece of nostalgia for the Twist just in case kids had forgotten about it while zealously prancing to the Pony. Checker sang, "C'mon, let's Twist again like we did last summer, yeah, let's Twist again like we did last year; do you remember when things were really hummin', yeah, come on again, Twistin' time is here." The record spent a dozen weeks in the Hot 100 between June and early September.

Remarkably, the mainstream recording industry, or the so-called "big six"— RCA, Columbia, Decca, Capitol, MGM, and Mercury — ignored the Twist. Despite "The Twist" having gone to number one, none of the major labels seemed to have thought the dance a marketable gimmick, for not one of them issued a Twist record in 1960 or in the first half of 1961. To the stodgy executives who ran these corporations, the Twist had been a flukish flare-up, a mere death twitch of the edgy rock and roll music they had tried so hard to wrestle to the ground a couple of years earlier. They were convinced that all this Twist non-

47

sense had finally blown over and followed the mambo, the Davy Crockett coonskin cap, and the Hula-Hoop into the black hole of history. They could now get back to the serious business of making the polite, polished, professional, and predictable pop music their shareholders preferred. As Chubby Checker's "Let's Twist Again" slipped off the charts, there must have been a collective sigh of relief in the headquarters of the big six. The Twist was dead.

Meanwhile in midtown Manhattan, less than two blocks from the Little Theater where Chubby Checker had introduced the Twist to America on "The Dick Clark Show" a year earlier, and a few dozen stories beneath the nearby soundproof corporate offices of RCA, Columbia, and Decca, there was a racket going on. The source of the din was a den of iniquity, a rock and roll bar, a hole in the wall on the litter-strewn south side of West Forty-fifth Street, just east of Seventh Avenue, adjoining the venerable Knickerbocker Hotel. It was called the Peppermint Lounge. If the record industry people had known about it, they would have called it a dump. They would have avoided the dingy interior, the sharp stench of spilt beer. They would have been intimidated by the working-class white toughs sitting at the bar in leather jackets. And their ears would have been offended by the loud house band, Joey Dee and the Starliters, pounding out rhythm and blues and Twist-rhythmed songs all night long.

Joey Dee, the handsome, diminutive leader of the group, had been born Joseph DiNicola on June 11, 1937, in Passaic, New Jersey. In the late 1950s, while he was attending Paterson State Teachers College, he put together an interracial R&B group: vocalists Rogers Freeman and David Brigati, organist Carlton Latimor, drummer Willie Davis, and himself on background vocals and alto saxophone. Several guitarists passed through the group, including a young Joe Pesci, who would later distinguish himself as an actor. When four black women whom DiNicola knew from high school began recording as the Shirelles for a local storefront operation called Sceptor Records, they graciously introduced him to the owner, a middle-aged housewife named Florence Greenberg. He and his band, Joey Dee and the Starliters, began their recording career on Sceptor in 1960 with a couple of doo-wop singles, "Face of an Angel" and "The Girl I Walked to School," featuring the lead voices, respectively, of Brigati and Freeman. In September 1960, after they'd been playing what one critic would later call "a good-natured imitation of rhythm and blues" around northern New Jersey, an agent named Don Davis saw them at the Oliveri Club in Lodi and offered them a three-day weekend gig at the Peppermint Lounge in Manhattan. "We just played Top Forty music, and the audience liked us," Dee said recently from his home in Seminole, Florida. "At the end of the weekend we became the house band. Our three days at the Peppermint turned into thirteen months."

The Peppermint Lounge had a battered, forty-foot-long mahogany bar in front and a rectangular dance floor with a small upraised stage in a back room that would have seemed too tiny even for changing tempos if wall mirrors hadn't reflected it into infinity. But as the Starliters's marathon dance jams began bringing in more kids, especially a lot of Jerseyites who had followed the band into the city to take advantage of New York's legal drinking age of eighteen, nobody seemed to mind the club's size or pedigree. As long as they could drink, Twist, and flirt, who cared? Each night the dreary watering hole turned into a palace of excitement and good times.

In the early fall, a few members of the city's aging jet set began dropping in. According to British writer Ren Grevatt, in the December 16, 1961, issue of *Melody Maker* magazine: "The publicist for the Peppermint arranged with Earl Blackwell, who is associated with a firm known as Celebrity Services, to bring some of his highly placed society friends into the spot. The idea behind this gambit was to gain mentions for the club in the society columns. This, in fact, is not an uncommon device when publicity is required. Often the idea drops dead. In the case at hand, it took fire fast."

One person lured to 128 West Forty-fifth Street was the *New York Journal-American*'s society columnist Igor Cassini — known as Cholly Knickerbocker. After watching one of his Russian-born aristocrat companions Twist in the midst of young barflies, he noted the experience in his "Smart Set" column on September 21, declaring, "The Twist is the new teenage dance craze. But you don't have to be a teenager to do the Twist." A couple of days later, Eugenia Shepherd, fashion columnist for the *New York Herald Tribune*, followed suit by mentioning that the Twist had become a specialty of the house at the Peppermint Lounge. Since the club happened to be in the theater district, Broadway denizens such as Truman Capote, Marilyn Monroe, Tallulah Bankhead, Shelley Winters, and Judy Garland started dropping in to Twist to the music of the house band and soak up the atmosphere. Noël Coward and the artsy gay crowd came to watch the sullen Peppermint Lounge lizards wiggle their slim hips. Local cafe society — the Duke and Duchess of Bedford, Bruno Paglia, and Mrs. Paglia (former film actress Merle Oberon) — abandoned the Stork's Cub Room (where rock and roll music was forbidden), El Morocco, the Harwyn Club, and the fading Le Club to slum with the Twisters. "Oh, darling, we must go to that dreadful place — everybody's talking about it, and anyone who's *anyone* will be there tonight." When Norman Mailer got out on the dance floor and moved around with Lady Jeanne Campbell (granddaughter of Lord Beaverbrook), columnists noted every twist and turn. By late October the national media, such as *Time* magazine, was stopping in to sneer at the goings-on and comment on the Peppermint's "low-level light, furred over by cigarette smoke." *Newsweek* noted that "the Twist, a rock 'n' roll comedy of Eros, has suddenly turned the Peppermint Lounge, a New York run-of-the-ginmill, into a melting pot for socialites, sailors, and salesmen."

Cholly Knickerbocker himself dashed off a self-serving recap of the fast-moving events in the *Journal-American*:

> New York Society was officially introduced to the Twist almost by accident. This columnist, with a group of friends, wandered

into a Broadway honky-tonk that bore the absurd name —
Peppermint Lounge. The place was filled with sailors, GIs,
young folks in sweaters and tight pants — they were all gyrating madly to the tunes of two fantastically lively orchestras. The
eternally young Col. Serge Obolensky, who was in our group,
joined the fray. The next day I wrote about it in my column.

This provoked a chain reaction. The very next night, a few
dozen socialites invaded the place. I wrote again about the
Peppermint Lounge and today it is indeed the hottest place in
town. NBC's "Today" televised it the other night and every
columnist in town has taken it up. The result is that now it's
tougher to get a table at the P.L. than at El Morocco.

The *New York Times*'s Arthur Gelb checked out the club in
mid-October and had this to say:

[T]he Peppermint and its surroundings are the scene of a
grotesque display every night from 10:30 to 3 o'clock. Cafe society has not gone slumming with such energy since its forays into
Harlem in the Twenties. Greta Garbo, Noël Coward, Elsa
Maxwell, Tennessee Williams, the Duke of Bedford and
Countess Bernadotte — often in black tie or Dior gown — vie
with sailors, leather-jacketed drifters and girls in toreador pants
for admission to the Peppermint's garish interior.

Patrolmen are bedeviled by a stream of limousines and
taxis. Passers-by are shoved off the curb or forced to elbow their
way through gaping throngs. The strident sounds of rock 'n' roll
pour into the street from a doorway reinforced by five bouncers.
The lure is a tiny dance floor undulating with the Twist. . . . In
the hot, jammed, smoky room, which holds 200 persons, patrons
were squeezed against the wall and bunched together at a mass
of small tables. . . . On the dance floor, couples gyrated in a joyless frenzy. They scrupulously confined themselves to a few
inches of space apiece, but everyone was being jostled nonetheless. . . .

Earl Blackwell, publisher of *Celebrity Register*, has reserved
a table at the Peppermint a number of times since he discovered
it about a month ago. 'There's nothing like this anywhere,' he
said with profound satisfaction yesterday morning. . . . Mr.
Blackwell is one of the favored dozen or so who do not have to
wait in line at the street entrance. He is privileged to enter the
Peppermint through a door in the [Knickerbocker] hotel lobby
that leads past garbage cans through a narrow serving pantry

and into the haven. . . . The saloon, which now turns away cus-
tomers by the hundreds every night, has no telephone listing.
Mr. Blackwell discovered that he could phone the
Knickerbocker Hotel and be connected with the Peppermint.
But it is pointless for anyone else to try to reserve a table this
way; a barmaid's voice will tell you, "First come, first served!"

The Peppermint Lounge may have possessed, in the words
of the *Journal-American*'s drama critic John McClain, "the
charm, noise, odor, and disorder of an overcrowded zoo," but
nonetheless it was now *the* place to be for the city's trendies
with too much time and money on their hands and a taste for
the cheap thrills of the demimonde. "For every motorcycle that
pulls up to the front door there's a Rolls Royce right behind it,"
Ira Howard wrote in early 1962 on the back of Joey Dee and the
Starliters' Sceptor album, *The Peppermint Twisters* — a mishmash of rhythm and blues instrumentals and the group's former doo-wop recordings, all overdubbed with crowd noises
and tinkling glass to make it sound live. "In the overflow line
that literally 'twists' around the block a full-length mink coat
alternates with almost every set of dungarees." The joint was so
jumping that one customer complained, "It took me an hour to
get a drink — even the waitresses were Twisting." But one of
the Peppermint Lounge proprietors, Ralph Saggese, took it all
in with a big smile and the wide eyes of disbelief. "It's like a
dream," he said. "One day I'll wake up and they'll all be gone."
(Saggese, an ex-New York City police captain, was one of the
club's three owners; the others were Sam Cornweiser, aka Sam
Cohn, and Louis Lombardi.)

Joey Dee told writer Wayne Jones: "There was always
excitement. Like there were a lot of vibrations because there
was a mixture of people. Like sailors on leave, MPs and SPs
knockin' them down and draggin' them out. That would create
a disturbance. You had the hookers, the bikers and the elite. It
was an unbelievable scene. The place only held 178 people and
you would think it was Madison Square Garden."

What fed the ongoing notoriety of the Peppermint Lounge

story was the press's fascination and puzzlement with the idea of the international jet set hanging out at a working-class rock and roll bar. There didn't seem to be a precedent for it in America, at least not since the twenties, when Prohibition made people do a lot of crazy things in a lot of strange places. But the Peppermint Lounge's sudden allure within the moneyed classes made sense in the context of a European phenomenon called the discothèque The word *discothèque* first appeared in Paris in the 1930s, a combination of *bibliothèque* (library) and *disque* (record) — a record collector's record library. A Parisian aficionado of *le hot jazz* widened the meaning of the word when he opened an underground nightclub in the late thirties called La Discothèque, where hip patrons could order drinks and pick their favorite jazz platters to be played by the bartenders on an expensive Victrola phonograph. Other discothèques opened around the city, and during the German occupation after 1940, when the Nazis banned American jazz, the clubs flourished behind inconspicuous doors in nondescript buildings on tiny back streets. In those dark days, sipping whiskey as you grooved to Louis Armstrong or Sidney Bechet in a discothèque was not only an act of defiance — much like Americans drinking bathtub gin and dancing the Charleston in speakeasies during Prohibition — but as patriotic as listening to "La Marseillaise."

After the war, in 1947, a Parisian named Paul Pacine opened a discothèque called Whiskey à Go Go. The "whiskey" came from all the labels of popular whiskeys that Pacine used to decorate the walls; the "go go" came from a popular American jazz expression, "Go, man, go," that Parisian hepcats used as a modifier meaning "more than enough" or "to spare." Jazz freaks flocked to the Whiskey à Go Go to drink whiskey and listen to either the jukebox or, on special nights, a disc jockey who played records on a phonograph, creating a mood from moment to moment with his choice of music. As the Whiskey became increasingly popular with local gentry, Pacine opened new Whiskeys in other major European cities. A Left Bank discothèque, Chez Castel, became one of Paris's most exclusive nightspots in the 1950s. By the sixties, the city's hottest discothèque was the very chichi Chez Regine, owned by a former ladies' room attendant at the Whiskey. The success of these clubs and their popularity with the jet set eventually inspired the first discotheque in the United States. Le Club opened its doors on the very last day of 1960 on Manhattan's East Fifty-fifth Street in the exclusive East Side neighborhood of Sutton Place. The disc jockeys there created an exotic rainbow of ambient hues by mixing French and Italian ballads with American rhythm and blues. One frequent visitor to Le Club, formerly a longtime regular at Chez Castel and Chez Regine in Paris, was former playboy Porfirio Rubirosa, one of the first of his crowd to discover the Peppermint Lounge. It was no coincidence that in the fall of 1961, when high society stumbled into the Peppermint Lounge and discovered that Twisting to the live music of Joey Dee and the Starliters made for a more exciting evening than listening to records, Le Club was already becoming passé and was only a few months away from closing.

Although Joey Dee and the Starliters had become synonymous with the Peppermint Lounge, their reign as the house band ended in December, just two months after the craze began there. "We'd been playing at the Peppermint almost every night for thirteen months, so we were ready for something new," Dee said. "Besides, we were being offered much more money elsewhere. First we did ten days for [disc jockey] Murray the K at the Brooklyn Fox [Theater] with people like Johnny Mathis, the Isley Brothers, Jackie Wilson. After that we flew out to Hollywood for a New Year's Eve party at Romanov's. I got to meet Governor [Pat] Brown, Jack Benny, George Burns, and Gracie Allen — all these people I admired. We went back to the Peppermint a few times after that to do one or two nights, but mostly we just toured for a couple of years there because we were having hit records."

The Peppermint wasn't the only place where the Twist was happening. Just down the street, an equally disreputable gin joint, the Wagon Wheel, had got in on the act and hired its own band, initially headed by Danny Lamego, playing familiar rock and roll songs at Twist tempos. (When the Starliters left the Peppermint Lounge, Lamego took their place and adopted the name Danny Peppermint.) At the posh Four Seasons restaurant, thanks to high society's sudden infatuation with all things Twisting, Chubby Checker was hired to appear at an exclusive Twist party fundraiser where 250 glittering muck-a-mucks, including Porfirio Rubirosa and his wife Odile, supermarket heir Huntington Hartford, and Henry Ford's daughter Charlotte, demurely wriggled and jiggled their tushes. History repeated itself when society folks went uptown to Smalls' Paradise at East 135th Street and Seventh Avenue, once one of Harlem's hottest jazz nightclubs. Gloria Vanderbilt and the Jacob Javitses were seen Twisting there in mixed company to the music of resident saxophonist King Curtis. "These white people come to Twist," said basketball star Wilt Chamberlain, the club's front man at the time. "This is the best Twist spot in town."

The Twist was also being seen at such functions as charity balls at Manhattan's Plaza Hotel and Mayor Robert J. Wagner's Victory Ball at the Astor Hotel. Portly society matron Elsa Maxwell giddily confided that Princess Olga of Yugoslavia had commented, quite off-the-record, dears, but I'll tell you anyway, that the Twist should only be danced at private parties. The fashion industry's $100-a-plate Party of the Year, held at New York's Metropolitan Museum of Art for 750 distinguished guests, hired Joey Dee and the Starliters to play Twist numbers all night. (According to Gay Talese, who covered the evening for the *New York Times*, the museum's director was outraged "when he saw photographers hastening to photograph the guests doing the Twist in the shrine of Rembrandt and Cezanne.") Even the Harwyn Club softened its anti-Twist stance and began a series of late-afternoon "Tea Twists," where perhaps the art of Twisting with pinkies extended was refined.

Before long, TV news was broadcasting fuzzy images of Mercury astronauts Twisting in zero gravity. Rob and Laura

Petrie, the young couple portrayed by Dick Van Dyke and Mary Tyler Moore on the then-struggling sitcom "The Dick Van Dyke Show," animatedly did the Twist; so did the animated Fred and Wilma Flintstone. Satin-voiced Nat King Cole reassured Americans that the craze hadn't crazed everyone as he sang "I Won't Twist" on Dinah Shore's popular NBC television variety show. At the movies, James Bond (Sean Connery) maneuvered on a Jamaican dance floor to a tinny instrumental called "Twisting with James" in *Dr. No*, the first of the popular 007 series. On Broadway, Hal March, star of *Come Blow Your Horn*, substituted the Twist in a scene in which he had been dancing a cha-cha. Bob Hope told a captive flock of airmen at advanced-warning radar bases in the Arctic Circle: "A guy froze to death doing the Twist; they couldn't bury him, they had to screw him in the ground." On New Year's Eve, while Twisters rang in 1962 at the first National Twist Contest, held in Louisville, Kentucky's Freedom Hall, columnist Earl Wilson in New York City declared: "If we hadn't had the Twist, 1961 would have been a bad year."

Consequently, all across America, the parents of the kids who'd made the Twist a hit in 1960 felt it was proper and time to try their hands, not to mention their hips and knees, at it. To Twist or not to Twist was no longer a valid litmus test as to who was scandalous, daring, or merely adventuresome. "I hear people saying it is sexy, but of course it isn't," said Elsa Maxwell. "It's too tiring to be sexy." Media guru Marshall McLuhan declared the new dance medium "very cool, very casual, like conversation without words," as well as "very unsexy." And media psychologist Dr. Albert Ellis pronounced, "There is sex implied in it — no doubt about that. But it's not a social sex urge. The sex image is confused to the individual; the partner might as well be a post." The nation's dance teacher, Arthur Murray, who went on record as saying, "The Twist is good for people who like to show off," offered the twist to the masses in "six easy lessons" for only twenty-five dollars; the more well heeled took instructions from Killer Joe Piro, a forty-one-year-old ex-Jitterbug champ and mambo teacher from the Palladium Ballroom who had taken up residence at the Peppermint Lounge. All this flurry prompted *Newsweek*, which in those days was not a sycophant to the entertainment industry, to comment: "In a few brief months the Twist has become more than a dance; it has turned into a national excursion into no-mind's land."

The acceptance of the Twist by Arthur Murray had particular significance at this point, because his august presence put the stench of highbrow amusement upon the Twist and signaled to every teenage social laggard that it was time to move on to something else. Murray, a sixty-six-year-old, horse-faced terpsichorean and professional fuddy-duddy stuffed into a perpetual tuxedo, had begun his career during World War I with Vernon and Irene Castle, a husband-and-wife dance team who hotfooted their way into millionairehood by opening several studios to teach common folks the latest society dance steps. When Murray started his own mail-order dance business in 1924, he was instantly successful due to his invention of the "dance mat," a folding map of diagrammatic outlines of feet and directional arrows that his customers could spread on their floors. Perhaps no other man in history had so many people following in his footsteps. Later, after Murray opened a chain of his own studios, he married his most graceful, elegant, and vivacious dance instructor, and in 1950 Arthur and Kathryn Murray became the darlings of American ballroom dance when "The Arthur Murray Party" began a ten-year run on television, imploring its audience to "Put a little fun in your life. Try dancing." The only obstacles standing between them and being the biggest squares on the tube were Lawrence Welk and Bishop Fulton J. Sheen.

When Kathryn showed up at the Peppermint Lounge, shimmering as if she'd just breezed in from a Park Avenue cocktail party, she told an observer named "Stanley" from the *New Yorker's* gossip brigade that she'd come "to learn and not to teach." As for her take on the Twist, Mrs. Murray considered it an exotic exercise for weight control, but hardly a dance. "No steps, pure swivel," her husband added with authority, but that of course didn't stop the Murrays's dance studio franchise from making a bundle teaching Twist lessons.

Not far from the Peppermint Lounge, the ballroom dancing purists at Roseland Dance City on West Fifty-second Street were not impressed with all this aristocratic fuss over the Twist. "It is not, in our opinion, a ballroom dance," said longtime Roseland owner Lou Brecker. "It is lacking in true grace, and since we have previously outlawed rock and roll as a feature at Roseland, we likewise will not permit the Twist to be danced." So there!

Donald Duncan, the editor of *Ballroom Dance Magazine*, concurred. He called the Twist "the biggest nothing dance of the twentieth century," but saved his bitchiest barbs for the hoity-toity thrill seekers who flocked to its temple on West Forty-fifth Street. "No doubt it *is* boring to sit around night after night in El Morocco or the Stork Club looking at the same old lifted faces. . . . Forthwith, like a cloud of chinchilla-clad locusts they descended upon the habitat of . . . the switchblade set." Fred Astaire pooh-poohed any notion that he might deign to teach the Twist at his dance studios. "Not me," he averred. "The Twist as far as we're concerned is just a body gyration with no set technique to be taught at this time." (He would soon change his mind.)

But as the Twist raged unabated, it picked up its share of highbrow defenders. Marshall Fishwick, professor of American studies at Washington and Lee University, tried not to be too pretentious when he called the Twist "a valid manifestaton of the Age of Anxiety; an outward manifestation of the anguish, frustration, and uncertainty of the 1960s; an effort to release some of the tension which, if suppressed and buried, could warp and destroy." A Philadelphia dance instructor praised the way the Twist "allows a lot more individualism than most popular dances. I think that's one of the reasons it's so popular. People are getting fed up with being automatons — whether it's on the factory production line or a dance floor."

In all the media frenzy, the original Twister himself, Hank

Ballard, who had moved to his new wife's hometown of Atlanta, Georgia, managed to catch a few rays of the reflected glory when former mayor William Hartsfield invited him to be the guest of honor at a $50,000 all-night soiree ball at the posh Piedmont Driving Club. Hartsfield took the opportunity to create the public impression that the Twist had been invented in Atlanta. Ballard was gracious and appreciative. "This is the greatest Twist party ever," he told the gathering.

In Los Angeles, where the epicenter of the Twist was the Crescendo Club on Sunset Strip until the Peppermint Lounge franchise, Peppermint West, arrived in Hollywood, the basic, unadorned dance steps came and went almost immediately, replaced by a dizzying series of variations: the Back Scratcher (the Twisters turn their backs to each other and pretend to rub against an imaginary pillar), the Fight (shadow boxing), and the Oversway (she bends backward and he bends forward, both as far as they can go). Four hundred miles north, at the Burlingame Country Club in fashionable Hillsborough just south of San Francisco, the swells adopted the game of Twisting with full highball glasses balanced atop their heads. Hints that they perhaps had water on the brain were not totally unfounded.

Hush-hush rumors had it that this Twist business could be traced all the way up to the Oval Office. The first whisperings that Camelot society had been contaminated began after Jean Smith, President Kennedy's sister, visited the Peppermint Lounge one night. Not long afterward, J. F. K. and Jackie, along with Jackie's sister, Princess Lee Radziwill, and fashion designer Oleg Cassini (Cholly Knickerbocker's brother), were reportedly seen Twisting like greenhorns at a black-tie party in the Blue Room of the White House to the purple strains of Lester Lanin's orchestra. The very idea of the sophisticated First Lady doing the Twist seemed especially unseemly, not to say shocking. Press Secretary Pierre Salinger firmly denied it, telling reporters that "I was there until 3 A.M. and nobody did the Twist." But the press was zealously on the trail.

Too zealously, it turned out. An Associated Press story that ran in many newspapers around the country raised more than eyebrows: "Fort Lauderdale, Florida. December 23 — Under a Secret Service guard, Mrs. Jacqueline Kennedy slipped out of Palm Beach last night and for an hour and a half danced the 'Twist' in a Fort Lauderdale nightclub [the oceanfront Golden Falcon]." *Horrors!* As it turned out, the real twist in the story was that the press spies had been following New York Senator Jacob Javits's niece, Stephanie Javits, who bore a resemblance to the First Lady. Appropriately red-faced, Associated Press president Benjamin McKelway wired an apology to the President and First Lady, and many of the nation's editors who had run the story did likewise. Miss Javits sent a note of contrition directly to Jackie, describing the adventure as "The first time I ever did the Twist in public, and it's probably my last."

Just as the Hula-Hoop craze had created a rash of stories about sprained joints and displaced vertebrae, the Twist began to generate news reports of hapless Twisters falling victim to muscle pulls and various strains of Twistitis. In November 1961, Dr. Bernie Davis, an orthopedic surgeon from Buffalo, reported to the *Medical Tribune* that he was seeing more and more knee injuries — the kind usually sustained while playing football — among Twisting teenagers. He'd operated on one boy to remove a piece of knee cartilage torn while twisting, and put a cast on a girl who'd dislocated a kneecap. The injuries, he explained, were caused by vigorous rotation of the knee, whose ligaments weren't designed to handle such lateral movement. "Under normal conditions, when excessive strain is put on knee ligaments, they react with pain and the person stops doing whatever is causing the pain," said Dr. Davis. "But in the Twist, teenagers seem to be hypnotized by the music and rhythm and don't realize the strain on the knee."

The Society of New Jersey Chiropractors, based in Linden, came out publicly against the Twist, branding it "a potentially hazardous torque movement causing strains in the lumbar and sacroiliac areas." And in Chicago, Dr. Carlo Scuderi extracted a bone fragment "the size of a 5-cent piece" from the knee of a fifteen-year-old. Another Chicago physician, Donald S. Miller, reported treating three back injuries in patients old enough to know better than to do the Twist. "People in their 40s and 50s should be more careful Twisting," said the doctor. Dance halls began to sport signs that read, Patrons Twist at Your Own Risk, which inspired Parkway Records to print a red and white starburst warning on the cover of Chubby Checker's *For Teen Twisters Only* album: Adults Twist at Your Own Risk! Perhaps the most succinct advice came from Marjorie B. May, home safety director for the Greater New York Safety Council. "Stop Twisting!" she said.

Bob Hope hoped to get in the last word (if not the last laugh) by quipping: "If they turned off the music, they'd all be arrested."

8: Put on Your Twistin' Shoes

> "The manufacturers of the B.V.D. Brand Sport Shirts have a group of shirts called the 'Twist' which they are promoting in conjunction with [the film] *Hey, Let's Twist.* This is an extremely promotion-minded outfit with thirty-six field men operating in 50 states; they are backing the *Hey, Let's Twist* tie-in to the hilt."
> —Paramount Pictures merchandising manual

When *Ebony* magazine ran a proud profile on Chubby Checker in early 1961, after the first wave of "The Twist," it showed a playful young man relaxing at home with his parents, driving around in his new Thunderbird, and scarfing down hamburgers and malts at a local soda shop. "I have to stay chubby," the two-hundred-pound singer said, blissfully ignorant of dietary admonitions. His manager kept him on an allowance of $150 a week, but Chubby was petitioning the court for an increase. "Right now, I never have more than a dollar in my pocket." That would change by the end of the year. His price would suddenly shoot up to $2,500 a performance, or $10,000 for a week's engagement, and the frenzy would sweat thirty pounds off his stocky frame.

Chubby Checker got his second wind on October 22, 1961, when Ed Sullivan invited him to come on his popular Sunday night program to sing a medley of "The Twist" and "Let's Twist Again," backed with a full orchestra. A troupe of twenty young dancers from David Merrick's Broadway production of *Do Re Me*, decked out appropriately in sweaters and bobby socks, slipped, dipped, and zigzagged all around him, dancing, as *Variety* put it, "a somewhat smoothed over and legitified version of the terp madness in broad and entertaining fashion." Parkway Records seized upon the Twist's newfound popularity by reissuing "The Twist" with a new, Kal Mann-written flipside, "Twistin' U.S.A.," replacing "Toot," but with the original 811 issue number intact. On November 13, "The Twist" reentered *Billboard*'s Hot 100 at number fifty-five—a sizable leap from nowhere.

With the reissue of Checker's single of "The Twist" came the selling of Chubby Checker himself. Henry G. Saperstein, president of a Los Angeles agency called Television Personalities, cut a deal with Checker's manager, Henry Colt, for a fifty-fifty merchandising arrangement that gave Saperstein the right to line up product endorsements. After all, Chubby Checker had inherited Elvis Presley's media mantle. As *Business Week* pointed out, "more than $45-million worth of products, including half a million tubes of lipstick bearing the name or image of Elvin [sic] Presley were sold in the past five years." During Elvis's 1956 media boom alone, forty-two manufacturers had licensed the right to sell Presleyana. So why shouldn't the same marketing strategy work for Chubby? This full-page, $6,000 ad ran in the *New York Times* in late November 1961: "MANUFACTURERS ATTENTION: A new nationwide name to presell your product . . . The Twist with Chubby Checker (the king of the Twist) who created the greatest nationwide dance in years! LICENSES AVAILABLE . . . BIG NAMES MEAN BIG BUSINESS."

The gambit paid off big. Makers of jewelry, hats, scarves, blue jeans, and sweatshirts called up Saperstein's New York representative, Harold Bell, to buy a piece of Chubby. Thom McAn shoe stores paid a licensing fee to introduce a new line of black-and-red Chubby Checker Twisters; "His Twisters" cost $8.99 and "Her Twisters" sold for less than half that, and Checker, complete with his imaginary towel, demonstrated in a television commercial how these new shoes somehow made your feet rotate better on the dance floor. H. M. Neckwear bought the concession to manufacture a cheap little tatter of hook-on cloth called the twist tie, retailing at one dollar. Benay-Albee Novelty Company got the nod to market a Chubby

Checker twist hat festooned with campaign buttons (filled with the image of Chubby's cherubic face) and a feather in the hatband (all for only a dollar). Empire Plastic marketed the Chubby Checker twister dance kit ($1.98): an old-fashioned foldout map with guiding footprints that looked like chalk marks the coroner had left behind after taking away several bodies found dead on their feet.

Bell, wary of dance-craze overkill, turned down toy makers: "We have a symbol, it's an image, and I think we would do harm to our image to get the pre-juveniles in on it," he said. Saperstein added that they were limiting their merchandising contracts to twenty because, "We don't take in much more money on fifty products than on twenty. And there's just so much space available at a counter for Chubby Checker merchandise." Saperstein and Checker also coproduced a line of ten one-minute twist instruction films, which were also edited into several Duncan Hines Fudge Mix five-minute "mini-specials" called "For Twisters Only." These syndicated programs aired in several of the larger TV markets around the country.

Most businesses simply did an end run around Chubby Checker by capitalizing on the popularity of the Twist itself. Clothing stores advertised "fashions with a twist," and Gimbel's Department Store offered a sale on its Twisteroo wool caps trimmed with fur (only $3.98) and a fringed, peppermint-striped twister dress ($5.99). "Anything with a fringe sells to Twisters," one clerk said, because twisting with fringed clothing, especially horizontal fringes on the hips, created an oscillating effect that gave a dancer more visual mileage out of every shake, shiver, and shimmy. Saks Fifth Avenue advertised black slacks fringed vertically from top to bottom. Fringes were nothing new — the Charleston-kicking flappers had worn them in the Roaring Twenties — but every generation reinvents at least one wheel. There were also Twist garters, cuff links, sweaters — even a Twist girdle. ("It's the dance that's dazzling the clubs from the East Side to the West Side," claimed the Abraham & Strauss department store in a large *New York Times* ad. "And

A&S knows what The Twist needs 'neath it all . . . Party girdles that twist with you . . . not on you!")

Beauty parlors suggested either Twist bangs (a natural forehead fringe) or the Twist—"a spiral upsweep coiffure," first seen atop actress Janet Leigh, that jounced without springing a curl while you danced all night. When Darby Shoes couldn't unload their line of flat-heeled moccasins, they advertised the shoes as "Twisters" and sold 15,000 pairs. Valentine Dolls in New York retooled one of its standard Barbie clones into the fringe-bedecked "Twisteen Action Doll" ($3.98). Health clubs announced their new "Twist off those extra pounds" classes. A frankfurter manufacturer began selling Twist hot dogs, and a Brooklyn pasta company developed a spaghetti line called the Twist. One furniture designer came up with a corkscrew-shaped Twist Chair, a "four-legged wrought-iron dance instructor" that could not be sat upon unless you squirmed and twisted your body into it. After devising the right ad campaign, Manhattan tobacconist Nat Sherman even emptied out his formerly slow-moving inventory of twisted stogies. "They really sell," he told a reporter after the name change.

On January 13, 1962, Chubby Checker's "The Twist" made history when it returned to the number-one spot on *Billboard*'s Hot 100 and hung on there for two weeks. No other pop record had ever gone to the top of the charts twice. It might have stayed there longer if Joey Dee's "Peppermint Twist—Part 1" hadn't pushed it aside and stayed three additional weeks at number one.

9: The Name of the Dance Is the Peppermint Twist

"Meet me, baby, down on Forty-fifth Street, where the Peppermint Twisters meet."
—Joey Dee and the Starliters, "Peppermint Twist"

Henry Glover, the dapper music arranger who'd written "Teardrops on Your Letter" and produced Hank Ballard's original "The Twist," was a musician from the old school and a legend in his own right. Born in Hot Springs, Arkansas, in 1922, he broke into the business writing arrangements for the Jimmie Lunceford Orchestra, one of the top black bands of the swing era, while he was studying for his master's degree at Detroit's Wayne State University. Glover later played trumpet with the Lucky Millinder and Tiny Bradshaw orchestras, and after he became Syd Nathan's right-hand man at King Records in 1947, he brought Millinder and Bradshaw to the label with him, along with their vocalists, Ben "Bull Moose" Jackson and Wynonie Harris. For Harris, Glover produced one of the most popular and far-reaching R&B records of 1948, "Good Rockin' Tonight." He also wrote several of Harris's hits, such as "Mr. Blues Is Coming to Town" and "Keep On Churnin' (Till the Butter Comes)," whose lasciviousness inspired Hank Ballard's later "Annie" records (one of which, "Annie Had a Baby," was cowritten by Glover). For Bull Moose Jackson, Henry Glover arranged and produced King Records' first major pop hit, "I Love You, Yes I Do," in 1948, and "Big Ten Inch Record"—which today remains one of the most popular early rhythm and blues "dirty" recordings. The biggest hit that Glover cowrote and produced at King was pianist Bill Doggett's million-selling 1956 instrumental, "Honky Tonk." That same year, Ray Charles recorded a number-one rhythm and blues version of

Glover's "Drown in My Own Tears," a prelude to "Teardrops on Your Letter."

By 1961, Henry Glover was working in New York for Roulette Records. Having misjudged "The Twist" as a mere B-side while producing Hank Ballard in Cincinnati, he was not about to let this dance phenomenon slip away from him again. "I found Joey Dee at the Peppermint Lounge in New York City and wrote and recorded the 'Peppermint Twist' with him at the height of the Twist craze," Glover told writer Arnold Shaw in the 1970s. As Joey Dee remembers it, "When the Peppermint Lounge was really hot, all the labels were coming in—Capitol, Columbia, Roulette. I told Florence [Greenberg, owner of Sceptor Records], 'It's time to do an album,' but she had already cut some stuff on us and wasn't interested in doing anything new. Well, right after that, Morris Levy, the guy that owned Roulette, came in personally and told me he could have a record out on me in two weeks. I asked him, 'Where do I sign?' Two days later, on a Sunday afternoon, his A&R man, Henry Glover, came into the club and introduced himself. He was a wonderful guy, he turned out to be a great mentor for me. He sat down at the piano and said we needed a new song called 'Peppermint Twist.' He said, 'It can't be anything like Hank Ballard's song, it's gotta be different.' So he started playing this rhythm on the piano, and three hours later we had ourselves a song." The band recorded "Peppermint Twist" two days after that, on Tuesday, at Pathe Studios on East 106th Street, where they had already begun filming a movie called *Hey, Let's Twist*. "Dave Brigati sang it first, and I just sang background," Joey Dee said. "But Henry didn't like it, so he asked me to sing instead, and that's what we finally recorded." A week later Roulette released "Peppermint Twist" as a two-sided single, parts one and two.

The song, like the Twist, was simplicity itself. While a baritone saxophone burped and vocalists Dave Brigati and Larry Vernieri (who had replaced Rogers Freeman) intoned in background unison, Dee sang, "Well they got a new dance and it goes like this, yeah the name of the dance is the Peppermint Twist, well you'll like it like this, the Peppermint Twist." The chorus then took up Hank Ballard's original dance instructions: "Round and around, up and down . . . " At the end of the side, the band broke into a familiar "Hey-hey-hey-hey" chant taken from the 1956 song "Hey-Hey-Hey-Hey"—recorded by both Johnny Otis and Little Richard—which itself was derived from a 1954 Johnny Ace and Big Mama Thornton duet called "Yes Baby." What separated Joey Dee's Peppermint Twist from the regular Twist, though not expressed in the song's lyrics, were occasional circular motions of the arms in front of the body to break up their to-and-fro movement, and frequent leaps into the air—not so much leaping, really, but rather pulling up the legs and dangling for a moment while the arms and torso kept Twisting. It became the preferred style, at least for those young and athletic enough to spring into the air every ten or twenty seconds.

"Peppermint Twist—Part 1" jumped into *Billboard*'s Hot 100 at number sixty-eight on November 20, just a week after Chubby Checker's "The Twist" returned to the chart. The Starliters's single was followed by a hastily assembled album, *Doin' the Twist at the Peppermint Lounge,* filled out with murky tracks recorded live at the club. "The engineer hung one microphone from the ceiling and ran the [sound] board from the coatroom," Joey Dee said, laughing. "That's all it was. I thought, 'Wow, we're recording this cheap,' but when it came time for the expenses to come out of my royalties, believe me, it wasn't cheap." The most prominent instrument on these live recordings was Carlton Latimor's Farfisa organ, which more than any other instrument came to represent the Starliters's sound, and would carry over into the future when members of the Starliters went on to form another organ-based group called the Young Rascals.

Since the chronicle of the Twist is like an abridged and telescoped history of rock and roll, it was only natural that Morris Levy got in on the action. After all, Levy had something to do with the coining of the term "rock and roll" in late 1954 as a euphemism for rhythm and blues. More importantly, Levy, a stocky roughneck, was one of New York's fabled independent record company owners who built the rock and roll business in his ruthless image. His label, Roulette Records, owned the masters of many of the early classic artists; his publishing company, Big Seven, owned their songs; and Levy made it a matter of principle that nobody got paid if he could help it.

Born into poverty on August 27, 1927, and raised in a tough Bronx neighborhood, Moishe Levy dropped out of school after assaulting his sixth-grade teacher, took odd jobs to support his widowed mother, and found his niche working in the photo darkrooms and hatcheck rooms of a couple of the city's nightclubs, where he met many friends who would later be of use to him. One was Tommy Eboli, a future partner in one of Levy's record companies and the alleged boss of the powerful Genovese crime family until his gangland murder in 1972; another was young Vince Gigante, who would ultimately become Vincent "the Chin" Gigante, the godfather of the Genovese family several years after Eboli's death. Levy made no secret of his Mafia associations. "When I was fourteen or fifteen I worked for people that were in the Mob because they were the people that owned the clubs," he told writers Justine Picardie and Dorothy Wade before his death in 1990. "They liked me because I was smart, I was hard-working, and I was a tough kid."

Barely out of his teens, Morris Levy took over the famous Birdland Club on Broadway from mobster Joseph "Joe the Wop" Cataldo. It was the first of many enterprises he fronted for similar silent partners. He also began his own music publishing company and dabbled in talent management. In 1954 he took over the personal management of Cleveland disc jockey Alan Freed and brought him to New York to preside over the city's nascent rhythm and blues revolution at station WINS. Levy was on hand at P.J. Moriarty's, a Broadway restaurant, when Freed decided to call his radio program "The Rock & Roll Show," and he conspired with Freed to copyright the name and collect royalties every time the term "rock & roll" was used. For a brief time he exacted fees from several small record operations that printed the catchy new phrase on their album covers, but when larger companies objected, Levy's copyright didn't hold up. A local judge declared that "rock & roll" in its various spellings had become generic. Still, rock and roll provided Morris Levy with other avenues for profit. Alan Freed's concerts brought in obscene amounts of money, as did the royalties on hit songs, such as Frankie Lymon's "Why Do Fools Fall in Love," that bore Levy's name as "composer." And of course Levy was there to assist Freed in honing the fine art of payola. He admitted many years later that he had put together "the best payola system in the United States."

In 1957 Levy launched his own label, Roulette, and almost immediately had a number-one hit with Buddy Knox's "Party Doll." And through a series of debt collections he took over other labels: Gee, Rama, End, and Gone alone gave him the masters and the music of the Crows (whose "Gee" had been one of the first crossover rhythm and blues hits in 1953–54), Frankie Lymon and the Teenagers, the Chantels, the Heartbeats, and the Harptones. Many years later, in 1993, when two of the surviving Teenagers sued to get back some of the rights to "Why Do Fools Fall in Love," the judge asked them why they had waited so long. "Because Morris Levy was still alive," they told him. The judge needed no further prompting to award them their composer rights and over a million dollars in back royalties. When James "Shep" Sheppard, lead singer of both the Heartbeats and the Limelites and the composer of the hit "Daddy's Home" (before Levy took it away from him), was found beaten and frozen to death in 1970, most black artists around New York couldn't be convinced that Morris Levy did not have something to do with it.

"Morris liked me," said Joey Dee, "and I didn't have any personal problems with him, but like everybody else I found him to be a tough businessman. He had a reputation for not paying anybody. I made some money from him, maybe more than most, but I know we should've gotten a lot more. My contract said I was supposed to get four percent, or about 3.6 cents for every [single], but after you deduct studio costs, promotional costs, well, there wasn't much left."

One thing that Joey Dee and the Starliters had going for them, in addition to being in the right place at the right time and under the beneficence of Morris Levy's "payola system," was a sound utterly different from Chubby Checker's records coming out of Philadelphia. The Starliters' first Roulette LP, *Doin' the Twist at the Peppermint Lounge*, hung on at number two in the album charts for six weeks in early 1962 despite its low-fidelity sound; their second album, the soundtrack LP for their Paramount film *Hey, Let's Twist*, charted in the Top Twenty; and Dee's how-to LP, *Dance the Authentic Peppermint Twist*, with vocal instructions and the ubiquitous pullout diagram, also sold well.

10: Eee-Ahh, Twist

> "I learned it in one minute. All anyone has to do is stand in
> one spot, shake the hips and swing the arms. That's the basic
> Twist. From there you go crazy, if you want to go crazy."
> —JoAnn Campbell, to writer George Carpozi

The Twist was bigger than ever in early 1962. From Orono to
Orlando, from Fairbanks to Fair Hope, from Port Angeles to
Los Angeles, from Jacksonville to Jackson Hole, from Goshen
County to Ocean City, from Park Avenue to Parkersburg, West
Virginia (where your narrator was the geekiest high-school
senior on the dance floor), kids and their parents were Twisting
in gymnasiums, ballrooms, dance halls, auditoriums, armories,
church basements, skating rinks, bowling alleys, country clubs,
band shells, nightclubs, gazebos, living rooms, dining rooms,
bedrooms, even in bathrooms. For three weeks in February,
three Twist records—"The Twist," "Peppermint Twist—Part
1," and Gary "U.S." Bonds's "Dear Lady Twist"—occupied the
Top Ten. Everyone wanted to learn how to Twist, and the task
of teaching them was gladly taken up by recording artists of
nearly every stripe. When Billy Lewis on the tiny Jin label
begged "Show Me How to Twist," he received no help from
anybody. Not so Cameo Records artist Bobby Rydell, however.
When he pleaded "Teach Me to Twist," Bobby got the expert
himself, Chubby Checker, to give explicit instructions. Now
listen carefully, because this gets a little complicated:

BOBBY: "Chubby, teach me to Twist. Chubby, teach me to
Twist. Well if I don't know how, look at all I miss . . ."

CHUBBY: "Well just watch me now when I move like
this . . ."

BOBBY: "C'mon, Chubby, teach me to Twist."

CHUBBY: "Now, Bobby, it's so easy to Twist. Bobby, it's so easy to Twist; now join the crowd and loop-de-loop . . ."

BOBBY: "Like a hula without a Hula-Hoop . . ."

CHUBBY: "C'mon, Bobby, I'll teach you to Twist."

Now let's move on to the lessons: "Get a beat in your feet, and you twist 'em on the ground, keep your head in the clouds, and the rest of you goes round and round." Chubby soon sums it all up with a sparkling nugget of 'Enry 'Iggins logic: "The gist of Twist is chiefly in the hips." Finally, we discover the whole nefarious conspiracy behind this record: "If you listen to the lesson we've been puttin' down, we'll get the whole wide world Twistin' round and round."

Chubby's follow-up to the second go-round of "The Twist" in early 1962 was "Slow Twistin'," essentially another Twist lesson, but with modifications so that Twisters wouldn't get bored. Again, he had a partner to play off of, a local sixteen-year-old girl this time named Dione LaRue; she normally performed as Dee Dee Sharp, but she was not credited on "Slow Twistin'."

"Baby, baby, baby, baby, take it easy, let's do it right," Chubby sang to the slow, lazy beat, as Dee Dee answered, "Let's do it right." Why? "'Cause there's no no Twistin' like the slow slow Twistin' with you." How do you Slow Twist? "A little crazy motion is all you need," Chubby counseled. "A piston-strokin' motion, you don't need speed."

Parkway was so impressed with Dee Dee's performance with Chubby that they brought her back, reportedly that very night, to record another dance record, "Mashed Potato Time," which would sell a million copies, outchart "Slow Twistin'," and only barely miss going to number one. Dee Dee would become the label's top female artist, with four Top Ten dance hits, but in early 1962 she was still relatively unknown. Because of her youth, Dee Dee didn't fly to Los Angeles to reprise her role when Chubby Checker lip-synched "Slow Twistin' " in the film *Don't Knock the Twist* with another woman. Perhaps Parkway wanted to keep Dee Dee away from the Twist, so that record buyers could associate her with the Mashed Potatoes and its natural spin-off, "Gravy (For My Mashed Potatoes)," without confusion.

"Mashed Potato Time"—based on the melody of the Marvelettes' number-one 1961 hit, "Please Mr. Postman"— was another Parkway exploitation of an earlier dance and recording by a group associated with King Records and "The Twist." By late 1959, one of King Records's newest hitmakers was James Brown, who had begun his career a few years earlier as a Hank Ballard imitator. "I'd been doing the Mashed Potatoes for years but I'd never put a name to it," Brown said in his 1986 autobiography. "The dance had been around for years, kind of in the public domain, but nobody ever did all the things with it that I did." When he approached his boss, Syd Nathan, about recording an instrumental for King Records built around the Mashed Potatoes, Nathan nixed the idea. So, while James Brown and his band, the JB's, were touring in Florida, he took the Mashed Potatoes to Miami producer Henry Stone—the sometimes King Records A&R man who had recorded the original demo of "The Twist" with the Midnighters back in early 1958. "I knew him from my days at the Palms there, and we had talked from time to time about doing something together," Brown said. "Sometime late that year, 1959, I cut the band on '(Do the) Mashed Potatoes, Part One and Two.' I did the vocal part and then got a disc jockey, King Coleman, to dub his voice over mine so I wouldn't violate my contract with King. We put it out under the name Nat Kendrick and the Swans." Kendrick was the band's drummer. Released on Stone's Dade label, "(Do the) Mashed Potatoes," featuring Coleman's shouts of "Mashed potatoes, yeah . . . yeah . . . yeah," became an R&B hit in early 1960 and even dented the pop charts. James Brown later parlayed the dance into a small 1962 hit, "Mashed Potatoes U.S.A.," but not until Joey Dee and the Starliters combined "(Do the) Mashed Potatoes" with the Dartells' "Hot Pastrami," under the title "Hot Pastrami with Mashed Potatoes—Part 1," did the song become Top Forty material.

Both "Peppermint Twist" and the flipside of Chubby Checker's "The Twist" reissue, "Twistin' U.S.A.," represented yet another phase of the Twist craze: self-reference not just as a dance but as a phenomenon. The Twist was news, and the new Twist recordings commented on what was going on. "Meet me, baby, down on Forty-fifth Street, where the Peppermint Twisters meet," Joey Dee offered. Sam Cooke revealed that New Yorkers of all classes had hit the dance floor together, "Twistin' the Night Away": "Here's a fellow in blue jeans, dancin' with an older queen, who's dolled up in a diamond ring . . . man, you oughta see her go, Twistin' to the rock and roll, here you find the young and old, Twistin' the night away."

In "Do the President Twist," Lula Reed, in a duet with blues singer-guitarist Freddy King, sang, "I want to go to Washington, to see the president Twist; the Cabinet members they all insist." But Kal Mann took an even larger perspective when he wrote "Twistin' U.S.A.": "They're Twistin' in Cleveland, in Kansas City too, they're wailin' in Wildwood, in Pittsburgh and St. Loo. So, baby, get ready, I'm a-gonna Twist with you. . . . They're Twistin' in New York, in old Chicago town, in Hollywood and Frisco, they all go round and round, they're Twistin' on 'Bandstand,' so don't you a-put me down."

"Twistin' U.S.A." had originally been recorded by Chubby Checker for one of his early albums, and Parkway later put it on the B-side of the reissue of "The Twist" only as an afterthought to the Twist's resurgence. But the first hit version of the song was recorded by Danny and the Juniors, as their debut on the Swan label, now owned primarily by Dick Clark's former partner Tony Mamarella. Dave White, a member of Danny and the Juniors, recalled, "We recorded 'Twistin' U.S.A.' at Reco Studios over the same [instrumental] tracks that Chubby used — Dave Appell's tracks. In several different languages." After the single went on the charts they recorded new lyrics over the same instrumental tracks to create "Twistin' England." Their use of Parkway's tracks had its price, however. "About a year later John Medora and I were producing a song we'd written called

'The Fly' with Carl and the Commanders," said White. "One of 'em at Cameo, either Bernie Lowe or Dave Appell—I forget now—said they wanted the record. They told us, 'If you don't let us put it out with Chubby, we'll write our own and blow you out of the water.' So we let them have our track, and to my knowledge it was the only outside track that Cameo ever used for Chubby." White added that he had provided the track of "The Fly" with its constant flylike buzzing by recording Medora's electric shaver.

After "Twistin' U.S.A.," Danny and the Juniors came back with a novelty called "Twistin' All Night Long" in which they spoofed Chubby Checker, Fats Domino, and other artists doing the Twist. The gimmick had worked for Checker back in 1959 with "The Class," so why couldn't it work again? Freddy Cannon, the Juniors's stablemate at Swan, and a relatively unknown group called the Four Seasons made guest appearances on the record. "Freddy and the Four Seasons really did the impressions, not us," said Joey Terranova, another member of the Juniors. The single would be the group's final Hot 100 charter.

The appeal of "Twistin' U.S.A." was its use of various city names from all over the country; conventional wisdom suggested that civic pride would generate enough sales in those cities alone to make the record very profitable. Most likely it was inspired by a 1958 hit by the Nu Tornados called "Philadelphia U.S.A.," and, more directly, by the era's ultimate gimmick hit single, "High School U.S.A." by Tommy Facenda, a former background singer from Gene Vincent's Blue Caps. In late 1959, Atlantic Records released twenty-eight different versions of "High School U.S.A.," each one chock-full of local high school names delivered in a rapid-fire auctioneer's vocal over the same instrumental track, and targeted them at twenty-eight different record distribution markets—New York City, Indiana, Washington/Baltimore, St. Louis/Kansas City, et al. —where the schools were located. Promoters billed it as "The Amazing 'Local' Record That Is Sweeping the Country."

Though released under separate serial numbers — from Atlantic 51 to Atlantic 78 — the twenty-eight different singles of "High School U.S.A." were tabulated on the sales charts as one record. It peaked, coincidentally, at number twenty-eight.

In 1963, the Beach Boys carried on the line with "Surfin' U.S.A.," but that's another story.

11: They Call Me Mister Twister

> "The Twist came and screwed up my life. It did! I had to work years and years before people noticed that I had any talent."
> —Chubby Checker

From "The Class" in 1959 to "Karate Monkey" in 1966, Parkway released twenty-seven Chubby Checker singles, from which thirty songs (thirty-one if you count "The Twist" twice) entered *Billboard*'s Hot 100 chart. Twenty-one of them were Top Forty hits, and seven made it into the Top Ten. Besides "The Twist," Checker had one other number-one hit, "Pony Time," in early 1961. Nearly every record he made was some kind of novelty dance song or an updated children's rhyme ("Loddy Lo"). Robert Farris Thompson, writing for the *Saturday Review* in 1962, called Checker's voice and style "nondescript" and defined his music as "broken-down rock-and-roll, and since rock-and-rock is, in the main, broken-down blues, a sense of loss doubly dispirits the ear."

Chubby Checker has not fared well among rock historians, and his name has never been proffered as a candidate for the Rock and Roll Hall of Fame. The general consensus is that he was a one-hit wonder whose one hit was so stupendously popular that it lasted ten years. Chubby's recording career could hardly be called checkered, for nearly all of his top-selling records subsequent to "The Twist" were reminiscent of it: "The Hucklebuck," "Pony Time," "The Fly," "Limbo Rock," "Popeye the Hitchhiker," "Let's Do the Freddie," and, of course, his follow-up Twist records such as "Let's Twist Again" and "Slow Twistin' " collectively formed what amounted to a one-note fermata for dance fanatics. Chubby was the dance teacher shouting out instructions on how to do the latest (or most recently

rediscovered) steps, mixed with ample amounts of encouragement ("You can do it now!"). In that regard he was simply
building upon his very first record, "The Class."

The nature of his talent and the quality of his music made
Chubby Checker a singles artist. His best recordings, released as
singles, were meant to be listened to one or two at a time. But
since they were also designed to be danced to, Parkway
exploited the need of Twisters everywhere to buy albums for
their parties (at $3.98 a pop in the early sixties; $4.98 if the LPs
were in stereo) so they could Twist and Twist some more, round
and around and up and down, without having to stop every
two and a half minutes to wait for the next seven-inch vinyl
donut to drop down the spool. Of Parkway's eighteen Chubby
Checker dance albums, thirteen were related to the Twist. And
several of them were major sellers at a time when rock and roll
acts, with the exceptions of Elvis Presley and Ricky Nelson,
rarely sold big in the LP market. Clearly, somebody besides kids
was buying them. *Twist with Chubby Checker*, released during
the early flush of "The Twist" single in the fall of 1960, spent
forty-two weeks on *Billboard*'s Top Forty album chart, peaking
at number three. *Your Twist Party*, a "greatest hits" repackage
job that Parkway tossed on the turbulent waters to ride the second wave of "The Twist" in late 1961, spent six weeks at number two and more than two-thirds of a year in the Top Forty. (All
that kept *Your Twist Party* from being the top-selling LP of any
given week were soundtrack LPs of Elvis's *Blue Hawaii* and
Henry Mancini's *Breakfast at Tiffany's*, and a Mitch Miller
Christmas album called *Holiday Sing Along with Mitch*.) In all,
Chubby's ten charting LPs spent a total of 183 weeks on
Billboard's Top Pop Albums chart between November 31, 1960,
and early April 1963.

If you listen carefully to any of Checker's Twist albums, you
can hear the cynicism of the men behind Parkway Records. In
their defense it could be said that a Chubby Checker album was
made to be danced to, not listened to. Part and parcel of the
Twist, after all, was the one monotonous, steady rhythm from

track one to track twelve. In the great American tradition, Parkway simply packaged and sold what the people wanted: an album to provide a good half-hour of Twisting. Fifteen years later, disco producers (at least one of whom got his start at Parkway) relentlessly raised the monotony factor in dance music to an art, so who can argue with Parkway's philosophy?

But as a listening experience, a Chubby Checker album— take your pick—borders on the excruciating. Make no mistake, Checker's recording of "The Twist" was great, and "Let's Twist Again," despite having been written in five minutes, wasn't bad either. But these were simply good songs, so basic in their structure and so visceral in their appeal that an artist or producer would have had to apply himself to screw them up. A typical Checker LP was *For Twisters Only*, released originally in early 1961 but not a hit until Parkway reissued it a year later, during the Peppermint Lounge craze. Because Parkway did not have a regular stable of songwriters outside of Kal Mann (who tended to rework other composers' popular songs anyway), Chubby had to rely on rock and roll standards that had been dolled up in fringe skirts and red-and-black Twister shoes. Fats Domino's "Blueberry Hill" (originally a 1920s Tin Pan Alley tune), Elvis Presley's "Hound Dog" (a Big Mama Thornton blues from 1953), Jerry Lee Lewis's "Whole Lotta Shakin' Goin' On" (a 1955 hillbilly boogie by Roy Hall), Big Joe Turner's "Shake, Rattle, and Roll," and Bill Haley and His Comets's "Rock Around the Clock" were all given the Twist treatment on the album, either ratcheted up or slowed down to a Twist rhythm, with a few lyric changes to remind listeners that they were supposed to be Twisting. "Twist Train" was a remake of the 1952 Jimmy Forrest saxophone classic, "Night Train" (which in turn had been taken from Duke Ellington's "Happy Go Lucky Local"). Danny and the Juniors' "At the Hop" became a Chubby Checker announcement that everybody was "Twistin' at the Hop." Mann submitted a piece of fluff called "But Girls" as well as a confused number, "Mister Twister," that blended the melody of Lloyd Price's "Personality" with the Big Bopper's rap from "Chantilly

Lace" and the sexual braggadocio of the Dominoes' "Sixty Minute Man" ("They call me Mister Twister, the lovin' end, I'm a-Mister Twister, the workin' girl's friend"). Perhaps the worst cut on the album was Fats Waller's "Your Feet's Too Big," which highlighted Checker's deficiencies as both a vocal stylist and a Waller-style humorist.

Let's Twist Again was another hit album best described now as an embarrassment. The first track, Lerner and Loewe's "I Could Have Danced All Night" from *My Fair Lady*, was surprisingly not too bad a performance. Chubby made no mention of the Twist itself, for in 1961 established songwriters in "legitimate" music did not take kindly to rockers tampering with their lyrics, fearing it would damage their copyrights, and so Lerner and Loewe or their publishers refused to give the required permission for Chubby to sing, "I could have Twisted all night." But that didn't stop Dave Appell and his Applejacks from putting the song's melody on the wheels of a Twist rhythm. The second song was Kal Mann's "The Jet," a disguised remake of Chan Romero's "Hippy Hippy Shake" cornballed up with low-rent, outer-space sound effects aimed at creating a new dance, the Jet, that flamed out before it could even get off the runway. ("The Jet" had originally been released as a single in 1959 or early 1960, several months before "The Twist.") Other lowlights on the album included Chubby's rendition of "I Almost Lost My Mind"—mimicking not Ivory Joe Hunter's rhythm and blues hit but the cover record by Pat Boone; a fractured remake of the gospel chestnut "Dem Bones," boneheadedly retitled "Twistin' Bones"; and "Takes Two to Tango," a two-step into squaresville that probably would have brought a blush to even Pat Boone's cheeks. The only interesting inclusion on this album was a remake of "Ballin' the Jack" that brought the Twist full circle. When Checker in 1961 told dancers to "Twist around and Twist around with all of your might," few of them realized that the lyric was at least fifty years old.

Easily the worst Chubby Checker album of all was *Twistin' Around the World*, released in early 1962 to exploit the Twist's growing international popularity. Imagine "Hava Nagila" done as a Twist—in Yiddish! Imagine "Twist Mit Mir" sung in German to the tune of "Muss I Denn" (the song Elvis Presley crooned in *G.I. Blues* as "Wooden Heart")! Imagine Chubby giving a shout out to Australia ("Twistin' Matilda") or Greece ("Miserlou") or Italy ("O Sole Mio")! Most perplexing was the trite "Tea for Two," written by a couple of Americans in 1925; Chubby made neither an allusion to distant lands nor a foray into a broken foreign language. What linked it to the other eleven recordings on this travelogue LP? Was he singing about all the tea in China? Having high tea in England? Only after savoring the awfulness of the female background singers and Checker's earnestly overprojected delivery does it become clear that on "Tea for Two" Chubby must have been visiting Las Vegas, craps 'n' crap capital of the world.

Performing in one or two keys to one basic rhythm running through a dozen songs for thirty minutes would be a handicap for any artist. Being saddled with a mixed bag of calculatedly ridiculous remakes and junky originals would be another. But Chubby Checker had to overcome other factors arrayed against him as well. Cameo-Parkway was a creatively corrupt operation. Kal Mann, Bernie Lowe, and even Dave Appell never fully concealed their contempt for rock and roll, the Twist, or the gullible youngsters who bought their records. They were products of an earlier, very different generation, musically and otherwise. Mann, who nominally produced the recordings, admitted that while writing some of Checker's songs he was thinking of vaudevillian Eddie Cantor, whom he considered to be the cat's meow, if not the bee's knees.

Although Cameo-Parkway had been cranking out hits and making copious amounts of money since 1957, Bernie Lowe had not thought his company's music deserving of updated studio technology. The record industry was still releasing monaural singles in 1960, but it generally issued albums in both mono and stereo formats; Ampex's two-track stereo tape recorder had been on the market since 1954, and by 1960 three-track recorders were the industry standard. Yet, according to Dave Appell, Cameo-Parkway continued to use its aging one-track Ampex. When Appell's prerecorded tracks were transferred to Reco Arts Studio's tape machine so that the vocalists could accompany them, the process diminished the fidelity of the musical instruments by a generation and added low-level hiss. Also, the primitive conditions of the Cameo-Parkway studio conspired with the old tape machine to make the instruments sound compressed, tinny, and thin by the time they reached the final master. The drums popped like toys.

One interesting cut that gives an insight into Parkway's recording and releasing methods was a two-track-mono (early, unbalanced "stereo") take of "Slow Twistin' " with a Chubby Checker vocal track roughened by little coughs and muffled lyrics. The company carelessly included this recording on the stereo version of Chubby's *For Teen Twisters Only* album. In one ear the listener heard Chubby and the lead saxophonist—each most likely recorded separately from the other; in the other ear was the instrumental track, compressed as usual, and Dee Dee Sharp's voice, slightly indistinct. This recording of "Slow Twistin' " was obviously taken from a raw, two-track studio tape from Reco Arts, rather than from the mono master that had been mixed down for the single, and the fact that Parkway included this unbalanced recording, which is fascinating to students of studio engineering but to no one else, displayed a shoddiness indicating that it had been haphazardly tossed together at the last second and rushed onto the market.

At least a third of Checker's recordings were overdubbed with an annoying, cloying female chorus—the same women who screeched on Cameo's Bobby Rydell records—that sounded like white junior-high-school cheerleaders. But in fact, claimed Dave Appell, "They were black grandmothers in their forties and fifties. They had a young sound but they were gospel singers." The shrill presence of these Valkyries was proof positive that Cameo-Parkway Records had no allegiance to or affinity for rock and roll. With their "yeah yeah" harping, the chorus turned every record they sang on into a vinyl charm bracelet, suitable for pubescent girls and no one else.

Finally, Chubby Checker himself, though a serviceable singer on upbeat songs (and even quite good on well-crafted but monochromatic melodies like "Lovely Lovely" or "Hey Bobba Needle"), fell short of the status of world-class singer that the Twist had bestowed upon him. He often strained when a song called for elasticity, and his attempts at singing blues or R&B ballads were pallid. That is where Chubby Checker differed from the man he copied. Hank Ballard could put over a weeper like "Teardrops on Your Letter" with conviction and soulful grit that made the song greater than it was; Checker would have turned it into a facile lounge number.

Easily the best element of the majority of Chubby Checker's recordings was the Dreamlovers, a black North Philadelphia quintet that sang background for him when the Valkyries were away. Bona fide doo-wop vocalists, the group breathed life into just about everything they sang on and even salvaged such dreck as "Takes Two to Tango." The Dreamlovers, who took their name from the title of a Bobby Darin hit, were tenors Morris Gardner, Tommy Ricks, and Cleveland Hammock, baritone Conrad Dunn, and his bass-voiced brother, James Ray Dunn. One day in 1960, after recording for the local V-Tone label, they got a call from Cameo-Parkway. "We had submitted a tape to Cameo," James Dunn told writer Wayne Jancik in the late 1980s. "They liked what they heard and called us up. We went down to the label to record as a group, or so we thought. . . . What they had called us in to do was backups."

The Dreamlovers became Parkway's in-house group, singing on many Chubby Checker and Dee Dee Sharp recordings. Dunn said he even sang bass on the Dovells' "Bristol Twistin' Annie." But the group members soon grew tired of being anonymous voices on other people's records, and signed with the first company to offer them a contract. Their debut single for Heritage Records, "When We Get Married," became a Top Forty hit. And when they subsequently recorded for

Columbia Records, their version of "Let's Twist Again" was just as good as the Chubby Checker original. The fact that Cameo-Parkway made no attempt to develop the Dreamlovers, while it hyped Sinatra-style teen idols like Bobby Rydell, illustrated the company's disregard for rock and roll music and its single-minded effort to soft-sell saccharine to Dick Clark's love-struck TV viewers.

12: And the Twist Goes Round and Round

"In one week in late October record reviewers in the leading trade journals received eight different new recordings of 'The Twist.' "
— Ren Grevatt, *Melody Maker*

The Twist record genre had one basic commandment: Thou shalt not end Twistin' with a *g* lest ye be branded as unhip. Waltzing, yes. Twisting, no. Droppin' the 'g' showed that the Twist, though not a folk dance, was a just-folks dance. This American conceit went all the way back to Ballin' the Jack and Messin' Around.

One of the most remarkable effects of the Twist craze was how many different kinds of Twist records became Top Forty hits. They included "Twistin' U.S.A." by Danny and the Juniors; "Let's Twist Again," "Slow Twistin'," and "Twist It Up" by Chubby Checker; "Peppermint Twist—Part 1" and "Hey, Let's Twist" by Joey Dee and the Starliters; "Twist and Shout" by the Isley Brothers; "Twistin' Postman" by the Marvelettes; "Twistin' the Night Away" by Sam Cooke; "Dear Lady Twist" and "Twist, Twist Senora" by Gary "U.S." Bonds; "Twist-Her" by Bill Black's Combo; "Soul Twist" by King Curtis and the Noble Knights; "Bristol Twistin' Annie" by the Dovells; and "Percolator (Twist)" by Billy Joe and the Checkmates.

One artist who extended the life of his recording career by adopting the Twist was a skinny version of Chubby Checker named Gary Anderson. Under the name Gary "U.S." Bonds, he'd been having Top Ten hits since late 1960, including a number-one million-seller called "Quarter to Three." Born in Florida on June 6, 1939, Anderson had moved as a teenager to

Norfolk, Virginia, and formed a street corner doo-wop group. A local Italian-American producer named Frank J. Guida, who had been responsible for creating "High School U.S.A." in 1959, heard the kid singing one day and invited him to wax a new country song called "New Orleans." Hoping to attract attention to the single, Guida released it under the *nom du disque* U.S. Bonds, reportedly without consulting Anderson about the change. Anderson's first name was added to subsequent releases only because Guida's image-making had worked too well; when "New Orleans" became a smash, people thought U.S. Bonds was a group.

Gary "U.S." Bonds was a handsome, light-complexioned black kid who wore his processed hair in a swirling pompadour and cut quite a figure for the girls to swoon over. Like Chubby Checker, he was largely a product of packaging. His voice was so thin that Guida double-tracked him singing along with himself and then thickened the "duet" some more with echo. The real musical force on most of Bonds's records, besides Frank Guida's production savvy, was a jazz-R&B studio band called Daddy G and the Church Street Five that featured a raw, heavy bass drum–driven sound perfect for dancing.

Bonds's first records had become popular during the Twist's initial run, and they were eminently Twistable anyway, so it was only natural that by 1962 he dropped the pretense and recorded a couple of bona fide Twist records, "Dear Lady Twist" and "Twist, Twist Senora." "That came about as a result of Frank Guida's stint in the army when he was stationed in the [Caribbean] Islands," Bonds told writer Wayne Jones in the late 1970s. "He had brought back with him some calypso records that he liked. I can't really remember the names of them but both 'Dear Lady Twist' and 'Twist, Twist Senora' were actually done from those two songs. [The original calypso songs were "Ole Lady" and "Jump in the Line," respectively.] We used the same melody but changed the lyrics around a bit to make it sound more American and kept the calypso beat to it." Actually, "Dear Lady Twist," featuring drummer Emmett

"Nabs" Shields's double-bass drumbeat prominently in the mix, sounded more like a seminal reggae record than a calypso. According to Guida, the song was originally the single's B-side, titled simply "Dear Lady," but an executive at Laurie Records told him the intended hit side, "Havin' So Much Fun," was going nowhere, then added, "we should flip it." At that point, Guida appended "Twist" to the title. Both "Dear Lady Twist" and "Twist, Twist Senora" went to number nine on *Billboard*'s pop chart. Bonds, incidentally, appeared in a 1962 British film with Chubby Checker called *It's Trad Dad!*

Guida also produced another Twist hit called "Twistin' Matilda" with a singer improbably named Jimmy Soul. The song had nothing to do with the Australian "Waltzing Matilda," which Chubby Checker had restyled as "Twistin' Matilda." Instead, this "Twistin' Matilda" was another of Guida's many updates of a Trinidadian song. (He's credited with bringing the major 1944 hit, "Rum and Coca-Cola," to the attention of comedian Morey Amsterdam, who in turn put his name on it and passed the song along to the Andrews Sisters.) Guida also came up with the name Jimmy Soul, because "soul" had become a popular black buzzword in 1962. Soul was born James McCleese in Harlem in 1942 and raised in North Carolina and Virginia, where at age seven he became a preacher and gospel prodigy known as "The Wonder Boy." He later sang for a time with the Sensational Nightingales, whose Joseph Wallace gave the basics of "The Twist" to Hank Ballard. But unlike Wallace, who avoided the secular music world, McCleese longed for a life in rock and roll. When Guida found him singing at a club in Norfolk, the first song they recorded was "Twistin' Matilda." A year later, Soul would have a number-one hit with another calypso remake called "If You Wanna Be Happy," which celebrated ugly women, and then he went into the record books as one of the very few artists unable to get back into the Hot 100 after having a number-one hit.

The Isley Brothers—Ronald, Rudolph, and O'Kelly—from Cincinnati (where the original "The Twist" had been recorded) cut "Shout" in 1959 and "Twist and Shout" three years later. Even though the latter was their only Twist hit, the Isleys came to represent the Twist as a *black* sound. Their original RCA version of "Shout"—influential without being a big charter—was the first popular rhythm and blues record with an unabashedly full gospel enthusiasm, swelling with screams and whoops that reflected the brothers' early years as members of a spiritual group, and a four-square Baptist organ played by the organist from the Isley Brothers' church in Cincinnati. Despite its lack of any reference to the Twist, "Shout" was a perfect Twist record. Joey Dee obviously thought so anyway, because he turned it into a Top Ten hit in early 1962 at the height of the Twist craze.

Songwriters Bert Berns (aka Bert Russell) and Phil Medley were so taken by the Isley Brothers' "Shout" that they wrote a natural sequel called "Twist and Shout" to take advantage of the first chart success of Chubby Checker's "The Twist" in 1960. As luck would have it, Berns wasn't able to get the song to the Isleys because the brothers recorded for RCA and were limited by the company to the repertoires of prescribed music publishers. In the meantime, because he was working with Atlantic Records artist Solomon Burke, Berns handed his song over to Atlantic producers Phil Spector and Jerry Wexler and arranger Teddy Randazzo (later to be the star of the film *Hey, Let's Twist*), who were getting ready to record a black vocal group called the Top Notes in February 1961. "Twist and Shout" was added to the end of the session. Unfortunately, the chemistry between Wexler and Spector wasn't right. "Together, we created negative synergy," Wexler later told writer Mark Ribowsky. "We stashed [Berns] in the mezzanine, with the spectators, and we went out there and proceeded to murder his song. There's a thousand ways to make a bad song and only one way to make it a good one. We never caught the right groove, the right spirit." Berns hated the result. When Wexler asked his opinion of what they'd done with his song, Berns bluntly told him, "You fucked it up!" After the Top Notes' version of "Twist and Shout" stiffed in midsummer of 1961, Berns figured that the momentum had been lost, and "Twist and Shout" was a dead issue.

Then suddenly "The Twist" became popular again late in the year. He arranged to produce a remake by the Isley Brothers, who by now had moved on to the tiny Wand label. Berns, a veteran session pianist, provided the second "Twist and Shout" with a new arrangement featuring a Brazilian baion rhythm (then popular on the Drifters's recordings being produced by Jerry Leiber and Mike Stoller) and a more gospel-tinged percussion and brass background. "Twist and Shout" shook the charts in 1962 and has remained one of the most popular Twist songs of all time, thanks in part to a 1963 remake by the Beatles (which itself found second life in 1986 when it was used as a musical centerpiece in the popular film *Ferris Bueller's Day Off*). A Bert Berns–produced Isley Brothers album, *Twist and Shout*— containing such songs as "Twistin' with Linda," "Spanish Twist," "Let's Twist Again," and "Rubberleg Twist"—was and remains probably the most substantial Twist LP, rich enough to survive beyond the Twist phenomenon.

At first glance, Sam Cooke was an odd candidate for Twist stardom. By 1962 the twenty-seven-year-old Chicago-born singer with matinee-idol looks was one of the leading rhythm and blues stylists as well as a familiar figure on the pop charts. Cooke has been credited with being one of the first "soul" singers, imbuing black popular music with the melismatic and emotional elements of the old Negro gospel. In that regard, his credentials were impeccable: From 1950 to 1956, he was one of the lead singers of the Soul Stirrers, a popular and respected gospel quintet. But in 1956 he began to flirt with pop. His first non-gospel single, "Lovable," released under the name Dale Cooke, was simply a rewording of a gospel song he'd recorded earlier with the Soul Stirrers called "Wonderful," with all references to God removed; "He's so wonderful" became "You're so lovable." The following year Cooke recorded a simple song called "You Send Me," which similarly borrowed from his earlier material. It became the first number-one pop smash by a single black vocalist since Nat King Cole's "Too Young" in 1951.

In 1960, when RCA Records artist Jesse Belvin was killed in a car wreck, the company immediately signed Sam Cooke as his replacement. As it had with Belvin, RCA at first tried to turn him into a polite, jazz-hued pop singer, but Cooke continued to write and record for the commercial teenage market. In late 1961, during a visit to New York City, he decided to take on the Twist. "Like, one night I went to the Peppermint Lounge and just wrote down what was going on around me," Cooke told writer Don Paulsen in 1964. "Out of it came 'Twistin' the Night Away.' " Cooke had already had a 1959 hit with "Everybody Likes to Cha Cha Cha," so he knew he was on sure footing with another dance record. His description of highbrows Twisting and rubbing body parts with lowbrows at the Peppermint Lounge reached number nine on the pop charts in the early spring and stayed at the top of *Billboard*'s R&B chart for three weeks. It remains a well crafted, listenable shard of pop that stands outside the Twist craze. (British rocker Rod Stewart reprised "Twistin' the Night Away" in 1973; it made the U.K. charts that year and again in 1980.)

One of the oddest Twist hits was "Twist-Her" by Bill Black's Combo, a Memphis crew of country-music pickers enjoying a roll of hit instrumental versions of popular songs, including "White Silver Sands." Country artists generally avoided the Twist like the plague, but Black had been spending the previous few years in upmarket clubs and, despite his conspicuous lack of youthful glamor (he was thirty-six years old and a few pounds overweight in 1962), on rock and roll stages, playing for noncountry audiences. Back in early 1954, Black was wearing a yokel hat with the front bill up, blue bib overalls, and black polish on a front tooth, clowning barefooted onstage while he slapped a stand-up bass in a hillbilly outfit called Doug Poindexter's Starlite Wranglers. One day Poindexter's record producer, Sam Phillips, owner of Sun Records in Memphis, picked Bill and the group's electric guitarist, Scotty Moore, to back up a hometown greenhorn named Elvis Presley on his first recording session. Although Black initially believed that the Presley kid had little talent and less of a future, he became part of the trio that went down in musical history as Elvis, Scotty, and Bill. When Presley signed with RCA in November 1955, Scotty and Bill went along with him, though by then Presley's handler, Colonel Tom Parker, had reduced their role to sidemen and downgraded their royalty agreements to meager sidemen salaries. The growing disparity between Presley's fortunes and their own eventually brought the partnership to an acrimonious end.

By 1959 Bill Black was back in Memphis, servicing air conditioners to keep a roof over his family's head while he sought a few gigs at night for a new combo he'd put together. Luckily he ran into an old friend, Ray Harris, a former Sun Records rockabilly singer who had started up a tiny label, Hi, a couple of years earlier with several partners. Things hadn't gone well for Hi Records, and Harris and company were about to fold the operation when Bill Black and his boys, featuring John "Ace" Cannon on tenor saxophone and a black blues pianist named Joe Lewis Hall, recorded a catchy riff called "Smokie." Released in the fall as by Bill Black's Combo, "Smokie" sold well on both the pop and rhythm and blues charts and saved the label. Over the next three years the group actually enjoyed their most success as an R&B act—with two number-one hits—thanks to their gritty, sax-and-piano-driven sound and a marketing strategy (no photos) that kept their racial identities a secret.

When "Twist-Her," powered by a piano so high and distorted in the mix that it must have kept the recording console's frequency needle in the red zone, charted in the Top Forty in early 1962, Hi Records buttressed it by renaming and reissuing a 1961 album, *Bill Black's Record Hop*, as *Let's Twist Her*, and re-titling "Smokie—Part 2" as "Smokey [*sic*] Part 2 (Twist)." The label also reissued "White Silver Sands" as "Twist—White Silver Sands," and the record actually charted for two weeks in May 1962. From Bill Black's Combo, Hi Records and its new crosstown rival, Stax Records, embarked upon a series of raunchy, gritty, black-and-white instrumental recordings that laid the groundwork for what would soon be known as the Memphis R&B sound.

King Curtis's "Soul Twist" was another instrumental hit. Born Curtis Ousley in Fort Worth, Texas, King Curtis was by 1962 R&B's premier tenor saxophonist. In 1950, when he was only sixteen years old, Curtis joined the big time as part of Lionel Hampton's orchestra. In the mid-fifties, after he relocated to New York, he became a prolific session man. Most important to his career, Curtis signed with Atlantic Records and thereafter backed up many of its artists, including Bobby Darin, Chuck Willis, Ruth Brown, and LaVern Baker. His most notable rock and roll collaboration was with Jerry Leiber and Mike Stoller's Coasters—he was often called the fifth Coaster because his stuttering, delirious "yakety" sax provided a distinctive voice on records like "Yakety Yak" and "Charlie Brown." Buddy Holly was such a King Curtis fan that he flew the sax man to Clovis, New Mexico, at his own expense for a session there with a brand-new artist that Holly was producing named Waylon Jennings. And yet King Curtis did not have a hit record under his own name until "Soul Twist."

By 1961, Curtis was freelancing as a session man around town and leading the house band at Smalls' Paradise on Seventh Avenue in Harlem. One of his studio gigs early in the year had been playing for Phil Spector on the Top Notes' ill-fated original version of "Twist and Shout." Hank Ballard's "The Twist" was already in Curtis's club repertoire when Smalls' began to pick up the high-society overflow from the Peppermint Lounge in November. Curtis's sudden popularity with important people led to his being picked to record a Twist single ("The Arthur Murray Twist") and an album that were part of a joint venture between RCA and the Arthur Murray Dance Studios. The LP included Curtis blasting "The Twist," "Let's Twist Again," and "The Peppermint Twist" on his tenor sax.

The term "soul" had not yet become part of the national

music vocabulary when Curtis slapped it on another Twist single in 1962, and "Soul Twist" appears to have been the first rhythm and blues hit—certainly the first number-one R&B hit—to use soul in the title. "I heard him playing it at Smalls' Paradise when the Twist was big and all the wealthy white people were coming up to Harlem again," said Bobby Robinson, a veteran black record store owner and record producer on 125th Street who had previously discovered Gladys Knight and the Pips and produced a number-one 1959 record with Wilbert Harrison called "Kansas City." "He called it 'Soul something-else' [actually "Jay Walk"] but I said, 'No, it's gotta be a Twist, and you gotta let your guitarist in more with the riff he's doin', 'cause that's the song's hook, that'll make it a hit.' So we recorded it, called it 'Soul Twist' and the other side 'Twisting Time,' and I rushed the record out on a new [Enjoy] label to catch the Christmas market, and it did pretty good for us." The recording itself was interesting because, although Curtis was a famous saxophonist, the primary instrumentalist—per Bobby Robinson's suggestion—was his blues guitarist, Billy Butler, playing a bass-string hook that not only made "Soul Twist" sound as low-down as anything being played at the time in southern juke joints, but also pulled the tune down into a lazy, smokey groove that could only be called "slow Twistin'."

Another independent Twist hit, and one of the more unusual, was "Percolator (Twist)" by Billy Joe and the Checkmates, a number-ten charter. A xylophone, accompanied only by a guitar and drum, mimicked the burbling syncopation of hot water percolating to the top of a coffeemaker. On the record's label, "Percolator" was printed as the actual title, with ("Twist") on the line beneath it in smaller type, indicating that calling the tune a Twist was an afterthought. In fact, the rhythm of the tune was not conducive for Twisting. Adding the parenthetic description was purely a commercial move to cover all bases, for this was one of those catchy novelties that would have caught on with or without the Twist's assistance. "Percolator (Twist)" had its modern roots in the music of arranger-composer Leroy Anderson, who with his "Pops" Concert Orchestra gave the world such familiar tunes as "The Syncopated Clock" (1951) and "The Typewriter" (1953), accompanied respectively by the ticking of a clock and the clickety-clack of a typewriter. Maxwell House Coffee later bought the rights to use "Percolator (Twist)" in TV commercials.

The bio of Billy Joe found in some rock books states that he was Billy Joe Hunter, but Billy Joe most likely didn't exist. A look at the song's composers—Louis Bideu and Ernie Freeman —tells the real story behind the artists. Bideu, a former disc jockey known as Lew Bedell, owned Dore Records, the Los Angeles company that released "Percolator (Twist)." Ernie Freeman was a Cleveland-born black pianist and arranger who, like Henry Glover and several other behind-the-scenes men, was one of the true unsung heroes of rock and roll. Bedell's claim to fame was that he had discovered Phil Spector and recorded his group, the Teddy Bears, in 1958, but Bedell was a wheeler-dealer, not a songwriter or a musician. Most likely Freeman, who died in 1981 at age fifty-nine, was the sole composer. Incidentally, under his own name, Ernie Freeman also recorded an instrumental version of "The Twist" that cracked Billboard's Hot 100 for one week in early 1962.

Billy Joe and the Checkmates were actually members of Freeman's black studio band, responsible for nearly a dozen hits besides "Percolator (Twist)" under various names. The basic lineup was Rene Hall on guitar, Red Callender on bass, Earl Palmer on drums, and occasionally Plas Johnson on tenor saxophone. This assemblage of musical greats recorded anonymously as B. Bumble and the Stingers ("Bumble Boogie" and "Nut Rocker"), the Marketts ("Surfer Stomp" and "Out of Limits"), the Routers ("Let's Go"), and the Dyna-Sores ("Alley Oop"), to name only a few. Most of these musicians also played on Ernie Freeman's own 1957 Top Ten hit, "Raunchy." As Rene Hall explained before his death in 1986, "We'd record these records and if they became hits we'd have to put together a young white group to send out on the road and promote it.

With B. Bumble and the Stingers, after our first record was a hit, we found a young band out of Oklahoma to go around the country and front for us. That's why I always kept it all simple, so that whatever group we sent out could follow our records." With "Percolator (Twist)," which had no "live" appeal, the ruse wasn't necessary. Freeman played the xylophone, backed by Hall and Palmer. For these three veteran musicians, who collectively had already played on at least two hundred hit records, including the works of Larry Williams, Fats Domino, Little Richard, Sam Cooke, Ritchie Valens, and Eddie Cochran, "Percolator (Twist)" was just another day's work.

One twist hit was a sequel to a number-one record by a female quintet called the Marvelettes. Led by vocalist Gladys Horton, the Marvelettes got together as the Marvels while still in high school in the Detroit suburb of Inkster. They auditioned for Motown Records in 1961. When owner Berry Gordy issued their first single, "Please Mr. Postman," on Motown's Tamla subsidiary later that year, it became the Motown operation's first number-one record. While "Please Mr. Postman" was still climbing the charts, Motown's principal A&R man, William "Mickey" Stevenson, called the girls into the company's studio on West Grand Boulevard to discuss their crucial follow-up single. Since many artists are stopped dead in their tracks by the so-called sophomore jinx, it was important to keep the Marvelettes' momentum going with something that was hot. "The trend of the Twist was really going then," Gladys Horton said recently in Los Angeles. "You could be sitting there feeling blue, and the minute a Twist record came on your energy would just pick right up. It was a lot of fun. So Mickey asked us to listen to this new song he'd written [with the Marvelettes' producers, Brian Holland and Robert Bateman] called 'Twistin' Postman.' Motown wanted to keep in the trend. Well, we liked it, it was cute, and in a day or so we had it all wrapped up. The band came in—we recorded in the studio with them in those days—so by the end of the day we had the Marvelettes' next record." "Twistin' Postman" reached number thirty-four in

March 1962, and began the group's string of follow-up hits that lasted until 1968.

Cameo-Parkway did its best to exploit the craze it had helped to create. Television's "Cool Ghoul," John Zacherle, a popular, cadaverous Philadelphia-based horror-movie host whose "Dinner with Drac—Part 1" had been a major Cameo hit in 1958, did the Twist with his assistant, Igor, by wringing a mummy dry—"You grab the feet, Igor, and I'll twist the head." The Meyer Davis Orchestra, Philadelphia's premier society band, rerecorded Checker's "Let's Twist Again," backed by the "Meyer Davis Twist." Dave Appell and His Applejacks, who'd had a hit in 1958 with "Mexican Hat Rock," gave the old *hua-pango* new life two years later as "Mexican Hat Twist," which Chubby Checker also recorded. Bobby Rydell chimed in with the aforementioned "Teach Me to Twist," and the Rocky Fellas contributed "South Pacific Twist." Cameo's Carroll Brothers recorded the eponymous theme song for the film *Don't Knock the Twist*. And, since the company had the original instrumental track to Chubby's "The Twist," two girls harmonized a new vocal track to the song, and Parkway reissued "The Twist" by Little Sisters; one of them, ostensibly, was the girl referred to in the song by big brother Chubby ("You should see my little sis"). Parkway was now saying, "You should also *hear* her." Then there was Chubby's own "Dancing Party," in which he named all the hip dances, including the Twist—"Twist and shout till you knock yourself out . . . at the Twistin' party tonight!" He also called out to the Cameo-Parkway roster: "Is Dee Dee here? (Yeah!) Are the Orlons here? (Yeah!) Are the Dreamlovers here? (Yeah!)." The record charted at number twelve in 1962, providing the company's artists with lots of free promotion.

"Bristol Twistin' Annie" by the Dovells—Chubby Checker's label mates on Parkway—was a remarkable piece of work because it was a sequel to both Hank Ballard's "Annie" records *and* "The Twist," as well as a belated follow-up to their own Top Ten hit, "Bristol Stomp." To top it off, the melody was taken from Al Dexter's "Pistol Packin' Mama" saga of recordings going back to 1944. That would qualify "Bristol Twistin' Annie" as a sequel to at least four different groups of records, three in the title alone.

A brief history of the Dovells provides an adjunct to the Chubby Checker story on Parkway. A mostly Jewish quintet from Dee Dee Sharp's alma mater, Overbrook High School in West Philadelphia, the Dovells clicked with their second Parkway single, "Bristol Stomp." As the group's first tenor, Jerry "Summers" Gross, told writer Krazy Greg Milewski, "While we were [in the studio], this promotion man, Billy Harper, came in and said, 'There's this new dance going on in Bristol [Pennsylvania], it's called the Stomp.' Then he put on the Students' record of 'Every Day of the Week' [on Chess Records]. . . . They took the guitar riff from the Students' record and they added this minor chord. It became G, A7, C and D instead of G, C and D."

Gross said that despite the group's run of five Top Forty hits, "Bristol Stomp" was the beginning of a spiral of lost hope and friction that ultimately destroyed the Dovells from the inside. "[Parkway] pulled the reins, they controlled it," he told Milewski. "We had very little say. I don't know if you've ever heard the Bristol Stomp album, some of the tunes on that are so flat. We recorded that album in one day between the Howard Theater in Washington and the Apollo in New York. They called us in and said, 'Do these tunes.' They wanted them right there on the spot. Some of them are just horrible." On one song the entire group, especially lead singer Len Barry, was off-key. "He missed every note there was," said Gross. "Bernie [Lowe] walks in and says, 'Great! Man, it's got that sound.' That was the beginning of the end. . . . They rushed us in and out of the studio so fast just to get product out."

Gross was particularly disenchanted with the released version of "Bristol Twistin' Annie." As he recalled, "We did 'Bristol Twistin' Annie' twenty-nine times. By the time we got to the twenty-eighth or twenty-ninth time it was so tight and so together, the harmonies were so perfect. They put out the second or third take. It's off in spots, it's flat. I mean it sucked!" Gross added, "If you listen to the background on some of those records, even the big hits they had out there, oh, there's something off-key, little things that shouldn't be there that they would let slide. I'm a perfectionist when it comes to stuff like this. They just didn't care." Gross remembered that later he felt humiliated when Brian Wilson of the Beach Boys innocently stung him by saying, "I tell you what, you teach us to dance and we'll teach you to sing."

As far as Jerry Gross was concerned, "Cameo-Parkway was not what I call a professionally run company. It was quick turnover, get the product out, jam as much as they could down the public's throat and sell as much as they could. . . . Bernie Lowe's thing was don't go for quality, go for quantity. Throw enough up against the wall, something's going to stick." And stick they did.

Other record companies got in on the action and rushed out Twist records of all descriptions. In some instances, once-popular artists tried to reprise their own hits with a Twist twist, such as Wilbert Harrison's "Kansas City Twist," the Champs' "Tequila Twist," the Royal Teens' "Short Shorts Twist," and the Virtues' "Guitar Boogie Twist," a 1960 record reissued two years later as "Guitar Boogie Shuffle Twist." None of these recordings sold very well, nor did they deserve to. Other well-known artists attempted, rather feebly, to create entirely new Twists: "Twist On Little Girl" by Jimmy Clanton, "Limbo Twist" by the Wailers, "Florida Twist" and "The Spanish Twist" by Bill Haley and His Comets (from their Roulette album *Twistin' Knights at the Roundtable [Live]*), "Theme for Twisters" by the String-A-Longs (of "Wheels" fame), the albums *Twist with the Ventures* and *Ventures Twist Party* by the popular guitar group, "Neil's Twist" by Neil Sedaka, and, for the teenyboppers who wanted romance with their dance, Fabian whispering "Kissin' and Twistin.' " Perhaps the most unavoidable was "The Alvin Twist" by the Chipmunks (with David Seville), the era's biggest-selling gimmick on record. The great Bo Diddley, who had a reputation to protect, made a slight attempt to hide behind "Big Bo's Twist" by abbreviating his name to Big Bo.

The most shameless method of cashing in was simply to reissue old recordings with new titles. Vince Castro's 1958 Apt Records single of "Bong Bong" came out two years later as "Bongo Twist"—despite there being no reference to Twisting in the lyrics; the song also had a jerky rhythm that made Twisting difficult. Imperial Records, whose Fats Domino had inspired Barbara Clark's naming of Chubby Checker, doubled back on Checker's territory after it found an unissued 1956 recording in its vaults of Domino singing a tune called "It Set Me Free." Imperial renamed the song "The Twist Set Me Free," even though the lyrics made no mention of anything even resembling the word twist, and duly placed it, along with a couple of other renamed instrumentals, on a 1962 Fats Domino album called *Twistin' the Stomp*. The earlier recording career of TV actor Vince Edwards came back to haunt him after he became an overnight sensation as the title character on the medical drama "Ben Casey" in late 1961; tiny Russ-Fi Records reissued one of his appalling 1959 recordings called "Squeelin' Parrot" and rechristened it "Squeelin' Parrot Twist."

Modern/Crown Records in Los Angeles, an exploitation mill that brought the art of packaging cheesy cut-rate albums to new depths, recycled their 1950s blues material on such LPs as *Twist with B.B. King*, *Twist with Etta James*, and *Twist with Jimmy McCracklin*. Atlantic/Atco Records issued two definitely non-Twist albums called *Twist with Bobby Darin* and *Do the Twist with Ray Charles*, and even released an anthology LP of mostly early fifties R&B recordings called *The Greatest Twist Hits*, including Ray Charles's "Mess Around," the Top Notes' original "Twist and Shout" (the only consciously made Twist recording on the album), and Tommy Ridgley's "Jam Up" from 1954, retitled "Jam Up Twist," with freshly overdubbed voices shouting "Twist" and other encouragements in the background!

Phil Spector's Philles label repackaged some non-Twist songs by one of his girl groups on *The Crystals Twist Uptown*, and King Records repackaged a dozen Hank Ballard and the Midnighters numbers on an album called *The Twistin' Fools*. In Chicago, the Chess-Checker labels tried to resuscitate the careers of their former rock and roll stars with *Chuck Berry Twist* and *Bo Diddley's a Twister*. Jubilee Records out of New York recycled its doo-wop and rhythm and blues material on albums like *Twistin' with the Cadillacs* and *Twist with Bobby Freeman*. When Duane Eddy departed his old label, Jamie Records, in 1962 to go with RCA Victor, both companies released Twist albums: *Twistin' with Duane Eddy* (Jamie) and *Twistin' and Twangin'* (RCA). After tenor saxophonist King Curtis's hit recording of "Soul Twist" inspired an album with the same title, another record company reissued some old Curtis cuts on an LP called *Doin' the Dixie Twist*. On his own SAR Records label, singer-entrepreneur Sam Cooke used a little more discretion. He rewrote one of the songs he'd already recorded, "Meet Me at Mary's Place," as "Meet Me at the Twistin' Place" and recorded it with singer Johnny Morisette on top of the same instrumental tracks. There was simply nothing a record company wouldn't do to hang the lucky charm of the Twist around its artists' necks.

For those companies that were actually recording new material to meet the demand, the most obvious tack, established during Chubby Checker's early Twist sessions, was simply to take a song (often one in the public domain), give it a Twist rhythm, and add Twist to the name. A couple of groups did "Raunchy Twist" based on Bill Justis's "Raunchy." Mario and the Flips as well as Checker himself renamed the sax instrumental "Night Train" as "Twistin' Train" and put words to it. Buddy Knox's former group, the Rhythm Aces, recorded "Mocking Bird Twist." Ricky and the Saints marched to "When the Saints Twist" and Louis Prima called the old gospel song "When the Saints Go Twistin' In." The Jim Dandies induced Bertolt Brecht and Kurt Weill to do a couple of twists in their graves with "Mackey's Twist" (from "Mack the Knife"). And the Ventures twanged around the sombrero with "Corrido

Twist." A group called the Night Owls, on the Valmor label, simply recorded a collection of formerly popular rock and roll songs for an album entitled *Twistin' to the Oldies*.

There was of course the inevitable sheer dreck, oftentimes performed by some of the unlikeliest people. Flower-child poet Rod McKuen still doesn't want to be reminded that he recorded "The Oliver Twist" (with "The Celebrity Twist" on the flipside), and Hugo Montenegro would probably like to forget "Tarantella Twist." Most other schlocksters, such as Dave Ede ("Twistin' Those Meeces to Pieces"), El Clod ("Pedro's Piano Roll Twist"), organist Maximillian ("The Twistin' Ghost"), and Melvin Gayle ("Kruschev Twist") used aliases in order to protect the guilty. Frank Sinatra hated both rock and roll and the Twist because they had made him irrelevant, but that didn't stop his Reprise Records label from presenting "Moon River Twist" and "Tonight Twist" by Trinidadian Aki Aleong and His Nobles, or Sinatra himself from recording a piece of flapdoodle commentary called "Everybody's Twisting."

And of course there were the artists looking to have some fun with the Twist. "Snuffy Twister," backed with "Buffalo Twister," by Snuffy Smith and the Hootin' Holler Twisters, was one of the very few Twist records with any connection to country music. (Bobby Lee Trammell's *Arkansas Twist* album was probably the only Twist release by a rockabilly artist.) Bobby "Boris" Pickett, having already mentioned in his number-one horror-show novelty "Monster Mash" that Dracula was doing the Transylvania Twist, staked out the sunless confines of a local studio and recorded a song with that title. Other singles included spacey instrumentals called "Venus Twist" and "Orbital Twist" by the Spacemen, "The Twomp" by Terry and the Tags (an attempt to combine the Twist with the Stomp, a popular dance among West Coast surfers), another instrumental called "Surfer's Twist" by the Defiants, "Let's Do the Cajun Twist" by Randy and the Rockets, "Dribble Twist" by the Raging Storms, "Pretzel Twist" by the Demotrons, and Tony and Joe's "Twist & Freeze," a sequel to their recording of "The Freeze" from 1958.

Combining two of the dances that Chubby Checker had turned into gold, the Hi-Lites recorded "Twistin' Pony"—on the Twistime label, no less. Bob (Feldman) and Jerry (Goldstein) revealed that "Chubby Isn't Chubby Anymore." Canadian Chad Allen, later of the group Guess Who, wanted to know "Who Invented the Twist?" Vito and the Salutations, tired of it all, suggested "Let's Untwist the Twist." Gabriel and the Angels seconded the motion with "Don't Wanna Twist." The Zircons warned "No Twistin' on Sunday." A black doo-wop group called the Genies came down with "Twistin' Pneumonia." Percussionists recorded beat-heavy instrumentals like "Drum Twist" (Kipper and the Exciters), "Conga Twist" (the Revels), and "Percussion Twist" (the Stardusters). Most inevitable of all were the Christmas records, including "Mama's Twistin' with Santa" by Mark Anthony, and a lively and very listenable "Twistin' Bells" by guitarists Santo and Johnny, which reached number forty-nine on the pop charts in late 1960. There were also "Twisteen Twelve" (Tchaikovsky's 1812 Overture) and "Twistmas Twee Twist" by artists long forgotten.

Every record company, big and small, scattered upon the market cheap albums by anonymous artists whose jackets screamed TWIST! The majors, typically getting hip to a musical trend as it became passé, coughed up a sorry batch of 1962 records whose sole purpose was to snag the browsing, uninformed shopper who wanted to be *with it:* the Adventurers's *Can't Stop Twistin'* (Columbia); *It's Twistin' Time* by George Hudson and the Kings of Twist (Capitol); *Twist to Songs Everyone Knows* by Chuck Marshall and the Twist Stars (Decca); *Come On & Twist* by the Original Twisters and *Dixie Twist* by Mike Simpson and the Raunch Hands (Mercury); *Let's Do the Twist for Adults* by Danny Davis and the Titans (MGM); Billy Joe and the Checkmates's drummer Earl Palmer pounding out his own version of *Percolator Twist (And Other Twist Hits)* (Liberty); and Perez Prado's *Now Twist Goes Latin* (RCA).

Many albums and artists were designed to create confusion with the Twist's biggest hitmakers. Probably the goofiest were three new performers who carried on the Fats Domino–Chubby Checker line by naming themselves Pudgy Parchesi, Chunky Checkmate, and (to also cash in on the Peppermint Lounge's cachet) Tubby Chess and His Candy Stripe Twisters. Laurie Records, a white doo-wop label best known for recording Dion and the Belmonts, released an LP called *Twist Calling* by Chubby Jackson. (After the Twist died down, a Chubby Checker look-alike named Round Robin recorded several singles extolling the joys of doing a new dance called the Slauson, named after a street in South Central Los Angeles.) One of the most exploitative album covers was Carlton Records's *Danny Peppermint Twist*. The bright red-and-white jacket, complete with a peppermint stick, looked so much like Joey Dee's live album from the Peppermint Lounge that a buyer had to look twice to catch the switch. Inside, Danny Peppermint, née Danny Lamego, even sang his own "The Peppermint Twist" as well as Joey Dee's "Peppermint Twist"—two entirely different songs separated by the *The*. (In Great Britain, Lamego's record sold better than Joey Dee's.) Similarly, Randy Andy and the Candymen released two albums, *The Twist* and *Let's Do the Twist*; the second LP contained Joey Dee and the Starliters's old doo-wop recording of "The Girl I Walked to School." The Starliters's label, Roulette, took advantage of the new Peppermint Lounge franchise in Florida by recording *Twistin' at the Miami Beach Peppermint Lounge (Recorded Live)* by the 7 Blends. There were also singles of "Do You Want to Dance" by Joey and the Twisters and "Peppermint Twist" by the Twisters (without Joey). Amid all this copycatting, the most admirable restraint of 1962 came from a small label that issued an album by veteran Texas blues singer Peppermint Harris without making any connection whatsoever to the Twist or the Peppermint Lounge.

Other albums by nameless entities provided record buyers with footstep patterns and stick-figure diagrams to help the hopelessly uncoordinated learn the Twist. An example was Spinorama Records's *Twist: Volumes One & Two*, by an unremarkable black studio group called Robby Robber and the Hi-

Jackers. Not only did these little masterworks include "Hillbilly Twist" and "Birdland Twist" (the Peppermint Lounge was already taken), they gave full instructions "How to dance THE TWIST" on the back of the record jackets:

> First get the feel of the beat of the music, and twist your hips with a swivel-like motion. Never stop twisting throughout the whole dance.
>
> BASIC STEPS: Keep twisting, only this time place your feet about 14 inches apart. Bend right knee, but keep right foot flat on the floor, with weight on right leg. Keep twisting . . . now shift to the other side; straighten right leg, bend left leg and put your weight on left foot. Now practice by facing your partner making sure never to touch. Your partner does the mirror-opposite of your steps.
>
> FORWARD & BACK STEPS: Keep on twisting in time to the beat and put your right foot about 12 inches in front and flat on the floor. Shift weight to right foot then draw it back; put left foot forward and shift weight to left foot. Always bend the forward knee and keep your trunk upright. Repeat 4 or 5 times and then vary it with the basic side to side step.
>
> BACK TO BACK POSITION: Start from the basic position with your feet 14 inches apart. Now cross right foot in front of the left foot and a few inches beyond, then swivel into a back to back position. Your partner opposite does the same movement but crosses the left foot over the right. . . . Keep on twisting those hips, and that's about all there is to it!!!

Berry Gordy, head of Motown Records, announced the size of his ego by writing "Twist Ala [*sic*] Berry Gordy" for a rare Motown LP called *Twistin' the World Around* by the Twistin' Kings. Other songs out at the time were "Twist á la Cacciatore" and "Twist Italiano." For the traveling Twister there were "Twist Around the World," "Twistin' All Around the World," "Twist City," "Twistville," "Twist Down to Baltimore," "Twist Street," "Twistin' in the Subway Blues," "The Twistin' Inn," "Twist Around Puget Sound," "Twist Around the State," "Twist By the Riverside," "Twistin' at the Waldorf," "Twist in the Snow," "Twistin' at the Zoo," and "Twistin' at Little Big Horn." For curious and athletic dancers there were "Twist Calypso,"

"Twist-Cha-Cha," "Twist Changa," "The Twist Test," "Twist and Fly," "Twist and Freeze," "Freeze and Twist," "Twist and Twirl," "Twist and Wiggle," "Twist and Wobble Tonight," "Twistin' and Bumpin'," "Twist, Twist, Ooh My Wrist," "Twistin' and Turning Polka," "Twist and Yodel," "Twistin' on the Surfboard," "Twist or Bust," "Menage a Twist," and "The Twist to End All Twists."

There were several songs, such as "Twistin' on the Bandstand Show," that made references to Dick Clark's "American Bandstand," but was there a "Bandstand Twist"? Yes. Bandleader Les Elgart, whose "Bandstand Boogie" was the familiar theme song for "American Bandstand," cut a new version called "Bandstand Twist." Columbia Records sent out promotional copies to deejays but never officially released the single.

Finally, there were two different songs titled "The Chubby Checker Twist," plus "Chubby, Twist with Me," "Chubby Ain't Chubby No More," and the aforementioned "Chubby Isn't Chubby Anymore." Indeed, one could say in 1962 that "The Twist Bug Is Going Around" and "The Twist Has Taken Possession." The world had gone "Twist Crazy."

13: Don't Knock the Twist

"Production hurry shows, but obvious timeliness helps. Fun for the cultists, entertainment for the curious. All in all, a showmanly quickie trip to market."
—*Variety* review of the film *Hey, Let's Twist*

The second coming of the Twist in late 1961 spawned four motion pictures with Twist in the title, and they were all low-budget, black-and-white, old-fashioned, and awful. Three of them were conceived *and* filmed in November and hurried into theaters in time for Christmas—and the fourth was a sequel.

Twist Around the Clock and *Don't Knock the Twist* ostensibly starred Chubby Checker and were produced by Sam Katzman, who several years earlier had made two Bill Haley and His Comets films called *Rock Around the Clock* and *Don't Knock the Rock*—a convincing indicator of Katzman's creative quotient. (One of the musical stars of 1957's *Don't Knock the Rock*, incidentally, was Dave Appell and His Applejacks.) Sam Katzman, with a two-tone fedora pulled down over his bald pate and a soggy cigar perpetually protruding from his mouth, was the epitome of the Hollywood B-movie mogul and one of the film industry's true characters. The sixty-year-old, New York–born producer had made his fortune cranking out more than three hundred flatly lit and even more flatly acted quickies since 1932, when he made a Western for $9,000, including the $150 he paid to his leading man, a relatively unknown youngster named John Wayne. That same year, it being the depth of the Depression, movie theaters across the land had instituted the so-called "double bill" to bolster their falling attendance. Major studios provided the featured attractions (the A pictures) and "poverty row" operations supplied, for a low set fee, B movies, or programmers, to fill out the bill. These B movies stayed within rigid genres, avoided any complicated scenes that might require more than one or two takes, usually ran for no more than an hour, and had to be made as inexpensively as possible in order to break even. Sam Katzman's oeuvre in Hollywood's bargain basement encompassed several Bela Lugosi horror films, a series of Jungle Jim and East Side Kids movies, Captain Video serials, early science-fiction cheapies like *Earth vs. the Flying Saucers,* and countless swashbuckler and slave-girl epics. He headed off criticism at the pass by bragging at every opportunity, "Every one of my films made money," but his parsimoniously produced flicks were such an anathema to serious talent that Columbia Studios boss Harry Cohn, who signed Katzman to a distribution deal in 1952, reportedly kept his movie stars in line with the threat, "If you don't behave yourself, I'll loan you out to Sam Katzman." Nonetheless, Katzman, with his ability to crank out schlock quickly enough to turn a passing fad into a sweepstakes, was the perfect man to sign Chubby Checker to a contract the first week in November and, by adhering to all the shortcuts and formulas of B movie–making, have *Twist Around the Clock* on the screen less than two months later. In fact, Katzman delivered a work print for Columbia's executives to look at as early as December 8.

Katzman didn't understand any music that came later than Glenn Miller's, but he knew exploitation, and he knew that kids liked the Twist as much as their big brothers and sisters had liked rock and roll. His 1956 and 1957 rock and roll films had consisted of a few cutaway musical performances held together with plots so thin that teenagers at drive-in passion pits could disappear into the back seats and fog up the windows for twenty minutes without losing their place in the story. Typical dialogue was "Man, that's the craziest." One person associated with *Don't Knock the Rock* in 1956 said it took less than eleven days to shoot and cost about $40,000. By 1961 through 1962, only the budgets had changed. According to *Twist Around the Clock*'s associate producer, Kal Mann, "Sam was a wonderful guy who never lost money on a film. *Twist Around the Clock* cost $250,000 and took only seven days to shoot." Katzman brought in James B. Gordon, the screenwriter responsible for the Bill Haley films, to rework one of his old rock and roll scripts. *Twist Around the Clock*—the story of a young talent scout trying to get a stodgy talent agency behind his new Twist dancing act—featured Chubby Checker singing three songs, along with Dion DiMucci (formerly of the Belmonts) and the Marcels, a black vocal group best remembered for torturing "Blue Moon" into a number-one, bomp-bompa-bomp, danga-dang-dang, doo-wop parody. The rest of the cast were unknown, talented enough tail-shakers and actors who seemed to have wandered in from one of Katzman's 1940s films. But never mind. *Twist Around the Clock* opened in forty countries and did good enough business to encourage a sequel. "It made a million," according to Kal Mann.

Twist Around the Clock premiered in the U.S. in December 1961, but opened wide in January. In New York it was paired with *The Three Stooges Meet Hercules*, a Columbia C film loaded down with comedy that creaked as badly as the joints of the aging Moe, Larry, and Curly Joe De Rita. The best that *New York Times* film critic Howard Thompson could say about the double bill was, "Together or separately, [they] could have been a lot worse." *Twist Around the Clock*, he added, "is painless and surprisingly perky. . . . The several sequences given over to mass demonstrations of the Twist are lively, buoyant and limber. The pear-shaped Mr. Checker performs a couple of his corkscrew specialties, winding like a top." On the West Coast, the *Hollywood Citizen-News* noted that the film "is cliche-riddled, threadbare in story content, and so 'corny' in spots, I thought for a moment I was back in Iowa." *Variety* was a little kinder when it noted, "Most of the choreographic action is regarded from below-the-belt, which, of course, is where the Twist really comes on strong."

Don't Knock the Twist showed up four months later, in April, possessing all the cinematic charm and pizzazz of *Twist Around the Clock*. "We're in great shape on this, compared to the first

Twist picture," Sam Katzman told writer Rowland Barber during the first day of shooting at Columbia Studios. "Same shooting schedule—seven days. But last time we only had two days to prepare. This time we had two weeks. This time the writer had five days to write the script and a whole weekend to polish it." Then Katzman laid out the week's schedule: "We're shooting the big [scenes] the first three days—dance numbers, scenes with lots of people. Then we kill the musicians and most of the dancers and extras. Fourth day we shoot the exteriors at the [Columbia] ranch [in Burbank], then we're down to shooting the story, the dramatic stuff. After the fifth day we kill Chubby Checker, and the last two days we only need three principals, three character people, three bit players, and six extras, tops. We shoot the finale on the third day and the opening scene on the last day, and nobody gets paid for just sitting."

The story line of *Don't Knock the Twist* harkened back to an even more cut-rate film, *Square Dance Jubilee* (1949), which Katzman probably wished he'd produced. When a TV executive (Lang Jeffries, fresh from his starring role in a 1961 Italian costume drama called *The Revolt of the Slaves*) has to get his network's ratings up by the end of the month, he hires Chubby Checker to throw together a Twist spectacular. (The TV "spectacular" was the precursor of the "special.") Chubby calls upon his friends Gene Chandler (brought into the film at the last minute to capitalize on his number-one hit, "Duke of Earl"), Parkway's Dovells ("Bristol Stomp"), the Carroll Brothers (Cameo Records's latest act), Linda Scott (riding the crest of a hit single called "I've Told Every Little Star"), and Vic Dana (a poor man's Vic Damone). Meanwhile, Jeffries's girlfriend, a Twist fashion designer (Mari Blanchard, who'd costarred in *Abbott and Costello Go to Mars* a decade earlier), tries to get the FCC and the spectacular's sponsors to cancel the show because she's jealous of a shapely young Twist dancer, Georgine Darcy. The lowlight of the film is a fashion show in which Darcy and her male dance partner model Twist creations for all occasions —boy-meets-girl, the date, the wedding, even the honeymoon.

The film's topper is "The Salome Twist," with Salome dancing a veil-tossing Twist with John the Baptist. To set the tone for these silly theatrics, the opening shot of *Don't Knock the Twist* was a closeup of a tightly clad feminine derrière shaking and wriggling into the camera, accompanied by the first line of dialogue: "That's what I like to see, boy. America on the move." The film ended without even trying to resolve the love triangle that it had spent so much time developing between musical numbers. *New York Times* critic Eugene Archer dismissed the goings-on as "embarrassing duties" and noted that Chubby Checker and the other musical stars "manage to seem even more improbable than the principals." Even *Variety* had to take a few pokes at this dead-on-arrival travesty: "*Don't Knock the Twist* may not be the definitive work in the Twist prism, in fact, it may be to the cinema what St. Vitus Dance is to terpsichore. . . . It appears as if George Van Marter's sets for Katzman's initial twist-flick were never struck in anticipation of the follow-up."

Don't Knock the Twist was barely more than a shill for Cameo-Parkway, which controlled most of the artists and the movie's thirteen songs, and for the dozen or so merchandisers who had signed lucrative deals with Checker's manager-producer, Kal Mann. According to a Columbia Pictures press release:

> The Fred Astaire Dance Studios is alerting its local managers to tie-in with *Don't Knock the Twist*. Studio managers are being urged to cooperate with theatres in setting up local promotions such as dance parties, theatre exhibitions, local tie-up advertising, displays inside and in the windows of Fred Astaire Studios, contests, use of Fred Astaire Dance Lesson Certificates as prizes, giveaways, etc.
>
> More than 900 Thom McAn Shoe Stores from coast to coast have been alerted to *Don't Knock the Twist*, and have been urged to work with theatres in local promotions, window and interior displays, lobby displays, contests, etc. . . . all keyed to Chubby Checker's appearance in the new film, and the fact that Thom McAn Stores are the exclusive retailers of "Chubby Checker Twisters."

Fearful that word of mouth might not sell the movie, Columbia harkened back to time-honored circus ballyhoo and suggested other ways for theater owners to start a street buzz about *Don't Knock the Twist*:

> Work with your local disc jockey on a street bally that will promote your show as well as his program. Have an attractive young girl, or a young couple, walk around town carrying a portable radio tuned to the jockey's radio station broadcasting Twist music. Every so often, [the] disc jockey might spin a Chubby Checker recording of a number played in the picture; passersby who tell the bally the name of the tune as well as picture and theatre credits receive guest tickets. . . .
>
> Get a sound truck through town playing Chubby Checker recordings. Be sure credits are posted on both sides of the truck. . . .
>
> Out of cardboard make a large replica of a phonograph record, with the label carrying credits: "Chubby Checker in *Don't Knock the Twist*, State Theatre, Now!" Have a bally wheel it through town, stopping so the curious can read the plug. . . .
>
> Suggest a debate on the Twist for one of your local radio/TV panel programs, those in favor of the new dance to give their reasons to opponents, the cats vs. the squares. Let your newspaper columnists or music critic get into the argument and advance theories for the popularity of The Twist.

In short, sell this piece of crap before everyone finds out what a dog it is!

Hollywood's Paramount Pictures, not to be outdone by its Gower Street neighbor to the north, had turned to its own version of Sam Katzman, a schlockmeister named Harry Romm, the minute it heard about Katzman signing Chubby Checker. Romm lacked Katzman's crude sense of self-parody, but he knew a little more about music. As a talent agent he had been responsible for Frank Sinatra's first film contract, and the first movie he produced was a musical called *Swing Parade of 1946* for Monogram Pictures. By the fifties he was grinding out such exploitation fare as Louis Prima and Keely Smith's *Hey Boy, Hey Girl* and a couple of late Three Stooges movies, including *Have Rocket, Will Travel*.

Since Chubby Checker was already under contract to

Columbia, Romm grabbed the next best thing: Joey Dee and the Starliters. The official story that Romm, a modern-day Barnum, put out through Paramount's flack corps was that he had been losing at the race track one day in early November when he looked up on the board, saw a long shot named Let's Twist, and decided to lay a bet on it. When the nag came in a winner, he remembered that he'd seen something about the Twist only that morning in the *New York Times*. Convinced that a new phenomenon was at hand, he went to the Peppermint Lounge that evening and, during a noisy intermission, shouted in Joey Dee's ear, "I'd like to make a movie with this Twist craze—and you and your boys!" Before the night was out, the ink was drying on the contracts. Over the weekend, Romm's screenwriter, the suspiciously named Hal Hackady, hacked out a story about the Peppermint Lounge, and by the following week a twenty-day shoot was under way. Some exterior shots and a couple of interiors were filmed at the Peppermint Lounge, but most of the movie—about 90 percent, including all the dialogue scenes— was shot at the old Pathe Studios on East 106th Street. Romm patched the film together fast enough to premiere it by Christmas.

In New York, Paramount made *Hey, Let's Twist* the bottom half of a double feature with Jerry Lewis's *The Errand Boy*, a slap in the face that later prompted Romm to sue Paramount for a million dollars, claiming the studio "failed to use its best efforts to secure the largest return for the picture." *Hey, Let's Twist's* press kit said it all: "Six Twist tunes are an integral part of the warmly sympathetic tale of a father who tries to put his two sons through college with the profits from his little Italian restaurant. Business goes from bad to worse and the boys themselves take a hand, turning the place from near-bankruptcy into the phenomenally successful 'Temple of the Twist' it is today." The *New York Times* described *Hey, Let's Twist* as "terrible . . . a wobbly little mess" that "rates a ripe raspberry," but the kinder *Variety*, which usually looked for a silver lining, deemed it "tolerable" and "an all-right novelty."

Despite his inexperience as an actor, Joey Dee starred in the role of one of the sons. As reliable support, Teddy Randazzo, a veteran of two Alan Freed rock and roll movies from seven years earlier, was brought in to play Joey's older brother. Randazzo was one of the first of the handsome Italian-American teen idols of the rock and roll era, having begun his career with the Three Chuckles in the mid-fifties. To round out the cast, baby-blue-eyed singer JoAnn "Blonde Bombshell" Campbell, formerly a staple of Alan Freed's stage shows, served as the obligatory love interest, and Broadway stage actress Zohra Lampert played a society columnist who accidentally stumbles into the Peppermint Lounge one night and gives the club the rave review that turns it into New York's "in" spot. Since a few scenes of *Hey, Let's Twist* were shot on location at the club, Paramount's ads duly announced, "Filmed where it happens every night!" as part of its you-are-there promotional strategy. Meanwhile, ABC-Paramount signed JoAnn Campbell and recorded an album with her called *Twistin' and Listenin'*.

The Fred Astaire Dance Studios franchise, having bought into a tie-in with Columbia's *Don't Knock the Twist* despite Astaire's early misgivings about the dance, covered its bets by also linking up with *Hey, Let's Twist*. In every city with a Fred Astaire Dance Studio, the first hundred people who attended the local screening of *Hey, Let's Twist* got a free twist lesson.

The film's most hilarious tie-in was the Hey, Let's Twist Joey Dee hat, a Tyrolean cap made of peppermint-striped cloth "which has caught on like wildfire from coast-to-coast wherever there's Twisting—and that's just about everywhere." The ridiculous looking hat, sporting a white feather on top, cost ninety-eight cents. The discerning Twister, of course, also had to have his white Peppermint Twist tie, with a red stripe down the middle, attached to his red-and-white-striped Twist sport shirt, both from the famous BVD clothing line. Bethlehem Lynn Sportswear also bought a merchandising license for *Hey, Let's Twist*, even though its tasseled Janet Twist belt for ladies wasn't striped like peppermint candy. MacFadden Publications rushed out a thin paperback, *Joey Dee and the Story of the Twist*, to coincide with the release of the film.

The bottom of the Twist movie barrel was *Twist All Night*, distributed by American International Pictures, popular at the time for making beach-blanket bashes and cheap horror films gilded with Edgar Allan Poe titles. *Twist All Night*, shot at the Republic Studios in Studio City, just north of Hollywood, went through several backers and a couple of titles—first *Doin' the Twist*, then *The Continental Twist*—before its official San Francisco premiere in mid-December. Tenor saxophonist Sam Butera and the Witnesses performed several Twist numbers—including the Big Bopper's "Chantilly Lace"—to save a small New Orleans nightclub and raise the bail to get Louis Prima out of jail. June Wilkinson, a platinum, low-rent version of Mamie Van Doren who had gotten her start in *Playboy* magazine, played the love interest. "Dig the Playgirl sensation of the nation!" the lobby card announced beneath a picture of Miss Wilkinson's prodigious thespian talents bursting out of her three-sizes-too-small angora sweater. Attached to *Twist All Night* was a five-minute color film called *How to Twist*.

First screened on the West Coast as *The Continental Twist*—"See Louis Prima, Sam Butera and the Witnesses do the Continental Twist . . . The Hottest Twist of Them All!" blared the earliest ads—the movie was bad enough to get tagged by *Variety* as "a rambunctious celluloid rumble into which a slim, shopworn story has been loosely constructed around periodic outbursts of the new dance. . . . Berni Gould's original screenplay is a pretty lame excuse for several frenetic displays of the bathtowel wiggle, as sexecuted by Louis Prima, June Wilkinson, Sam Butera and a host of nervous torso wrenchers. . . . As a spectator sport, the Twist suffers from an element of monotony. Esthetically, it has about as much charm as an exhibition at Vic Tanny's [gym]." The paper's only praise was directed at "Miss Wilkinson's anatomical proportions [which] are admirably suited to the machinations and undulations of this holds-barred slice of contemporary choreography."

Like nearly everything else about the Twist, the films purporting to chronicle it were cynically produced, slapdash knick-knacks designed to fleece anyone momentarily blinded by the flash and trendiness, then take the money and run. When the Twist records faded into obscurity, all four Twist movies did likewise.

14: Twistin' All 'Round the World

"[The Twist] expresses dirty feelings, dirty instincts, and poverty of thought and spirit."

—*Izvestia*, quoting Soviet choreographer Igor Moiseyev

Beverly Nichols, a British entertainment correspondent, wrote from New York City during the first heat of Peppermint fever: "I'm not easily shocked but the Twist shocked me. Half Negroid, half Manhattan, and when you see it on its native heath, wholly frightening. I can't believe that London will ever go to quite such extremes!" He was wrong, of course. "They're Twistin' in London, in Londonderry too; they're wailin' in North Wales, in Leeds and Liverpool," Danny and the Juniors sang in "Twistin' England," their follow-up to their hit version of "Twistin' U.S.A."

In late summer 1960, the British arm of Columbia Records released "The Twist" by Chubby Checker in the United Kingdom. The single skipped into the Top Fifty chart of the British trade magazine *Record Retailer* in late September and again in October, but only for a week each time, and rose no higher than number forty-four. But when the Twist went from being a mere dance to being a craze, the Brits—and indeed most of the world—proved to be almost as susceptible as the nutty Americans. The first sign came in August 1961, when Chubby Checker's "Let's Twist Again" flitted around *Record Retailer*'s chart for three weeks. Then it returned in late December for a twenty-seven-week run, topping out at number two, after Chubby Checker arrived at London's Heathrow Airport for a British tour.

What awaited him was "frenzy, it was Chubby Checker mania," he said many years later, without modesty. "It was very much like Beatlemania, and it was very exciting for me, a young black man who was in his teens, to be really the first international superstar." This time, instead of having Dick Clark and tiny Parkway behind him, Chubby enjoyed the support of a major international record company, Columbia, which had bought foreign rights to his recordings. Columbia was a powerhouse in the small, tightly controlled British entertainment industry, and its support gave Checker and the Twist corporate legitimacy. Besides putting him on a music hall tour with mainstream acts, Columbia lined up appearances for him in a respectably made film and on a TV special.

Philadelphia native and London-based expatriate Richard Lester, still a couple of years away from directing the Beatles' *A Hard Day's Night*, had just finished shooting a rock and roll movie called *It's Trad Dad!* (released in the U.S. as *Ring-a-Ding Rhythm*) when "Let's Twist Again" and the Twist blitzed London. To widen the film's appeal he wanted a few more American artists, and he wanted the King of the Twisters himself. Columbia Records, already providing financial backing (and most of the talent) for the film, handed him Chubby Checker, who was due in London for a British tour in several weeks. But Lester couldn't wait that long. Instead, he flew to New York with his cinematographer, rented a studio, and filmed Checker singing and Twisting along with "The Lose Your Inhibitions Twist." Lester also filmed Gary "U.S." Bonds and Gene McDaniels. Hurrying back to London with his new footage, he put together one last scene at Shepperton Studios in which he filmed young trads, mods, and rockers Twisting, then intercut them with Chubby Checker's New York performance.

When *It's Trad Dad!* was released a month later, Columbia naturally used its press contacts to promote not only Checker and the Twist but the film's other artists. One of Checker's costars, British clarinetist Mr. Acker Bilk, made a big flap in the press about not being impressed. Bilk, whose mellow "Stranger on the Shore" was a number-one hit in the U.S. at the time, told *New Musical Express*: "I don't think the public is going to swallow this one whole. The Twist's success looks like being short but sweet. As you know we've got the dance in the film I just completed. The girls look great in action! But the fellas—plain daft! In America they needed a new craze—something to revive the flagging interest in rock and roll." Singing heartthrob Cliff Richard, also a Columbia artist, was a little more generous: "Sure, I dig the Twist. It knocks me out. Haven't quite mastered the thing I must admit, even though I did get some first-hand instructions from Chubby when he was over here. Only thing that bugs me is the constant reports I keep hearing from the medics. You know, all this about causing muscular contortions and spine injuries."

Chubby got top billing on a British variety TV special called "Personal Appearance (Trad with a Twist)." Trad, or traditional jazz (known as Dixieland in the States), was the rage in Great Britain when he arrived in late 1961, but in its review of the program's roster of a dozen mostly jazz artists, *Variety* focused on the American: "Chief guest Checker demonstrated the Twist with great agility and verve as he powerhoused through 'The Twist,' 'The Fly' and 'Let's Twist Again.' These numbers were so startlingly similar, though, it was difficult to tell he had changed them. . . . Apart from Checker, the show offered nothing new and could even help to cool off the trad fad with its exposure of so much unversatile noise from inexperienced lips." The reviewer wasn't far off the mark. Trad jazz may have already been on its way out the door when it shared the big and little screens with the Twist, but Chubby Checker gave it the bum's rush. By early 1962 the trad fad was dead, dad.

At about the same time as "Personal Appearance (Trad with a Twist)" aired, Victor Sylvester, Great Britain's "king of the dance floor" and host of the BBC's Monday night "Television Dancing Club," formally introduced the Twist to British society. As England's answer to Lawrence Welk, Sylvester was an important emissary for the dance. His son, Victor Sylvester Jr., told BBC Radio 2 documentarian Louise Bruce many years later: "We saw a telly recording of Chubby Checker, and my father made some inquiries and then decided to teach the basic steps. There were very few of them, it wasn't a difficult dance to learn. What everyone was trying to master was the sort of wiggle—I mean, we'd had the Hula-Hoop craze and it seemed to be rather similar, you had to sort of rotate your hips in a certain way." Sylvester's Ballroom Orchestra's "Fascinating Rhythm Twist"—the Gershwins's classic set to a mild Twist rhythm— sounded appropriately square and set grandmothers Twisting.

There was some resistance. A Mr. Stetson, who headed up two dancing institutes in London, banned the Twist because it was immoral. "The knees and pelvis are used in such a way that the dancer is making very suggestive movements," he told the BBC, his jaws audibly tight with indignation. He reacted especially to the Twist's narcissism. "I have an extreme objection to the fact that this is not what is called a couple dance. It is a solo dance. A girl can just as easily go out onto the dance floor without having a partner and exhibit herself in what I consider to be in rather an unseemly way for British ballrooms." In the months ahead this distressed dance master would need a stiff upper lip as badly as a supple body and nimble feet, because the Twist was definitely taking over the nation's ballrooms.

Another British dance show, running on alternate Mondays to Victor Sylvester's "Television Dancing Party," was "Come Dancing," where sleek-footed Lionel Blair and his assistant Joyce demonstrated the Twist on February 5, 1962. "I was invited to the premiere of this film called *Twist Around the Clock*," Blair told Louise Bruce. Already familiar with the earlier *Rock Around the Clock*, Blair was intrigued. "I went to see it and I met Chubby Checker afterward—he was at the premiere—who was charming, and he taught me in the foyer of the Columbia Cinema how to do the Twist." The film's promoters were moving *Twist Around the Clock* into London's New Victoria Theater across from Victoria Station, so they asked Blair to choreograph a semi-variety stage show that would segue seamlessly into the movie. "Right at the end of the dance routine it'll come onto the film," the promoter suggested. They did four complete shows a

day, the Twist became a sensation, and *Twist Around the Clock*—
"Full length and Twist-terrific"—did great business all around
the country.

When Columbia reissued Checker's "The Twist" in early
1962, it shimmied up the charts, followed by "Slow Twistin',"
"Teach Me to Twist" (with Bobby Rydell), and the rerelease of
"Let's Twist Again"—a song the British clearly favored over
"The Twist." Sam Cooke's "Twistin' the Night Away" was a Top
Ten hit. Joey Dee and the Starliters' "Peppermint Twist," also
released on Columbia Records, did relatively good business, as
did "The Peppermint Twist" (a different song) by Joey Dee's
Peppermint Lounge replacement, Danny Peppermint, billed on
his London Records release as Danny Peppermint and the Jump-
ing Jacks. Even Frank Sinatra, who had earlier lambasted the
Twist, felt impelled to comment on his own Reprise label that
"Everybody's Twisting"—showing what a hip guy he was by
leaving the participle's *g* in place. A Belgian group called
Chakachas, recording for RCA, got in on the act with a song
called "Twist Twist." Local talent tried to cash in, but with little
success. The biggest homegrown hit was Petula Clark's "Ya Ya
Twist." Frankie Vaughan, a popular British vocalist specializing
in recording remakes of American hits, had lukewarm luck with
"Don't Stop Twist," but the Vernons Girls' "Making the Most of
the Twist"—a cautionary tale equating a guy's natural Twisting
ability with twisting a girl around his finger: "Guys are natural
Twisters, you know what I mean"—couldn't compete with the
meatier material being imported from the United States.

The Twist's success in Great Britain was almost a foregone
conclusion because, to the British, rock and roll was (and is)
something excitingly American, like Western movies and comic
books. Also, they harbored none of Middle America's class and
racial prejudices against it. Many fifties rockers, particularly the
grossly underrated Gene Vincent, found mainstream stardom
in England after rock dried up at home, and Buddy Holly, following his death in 1959 , had a string of seventeen hit records
lasting throughout most of the sixties. To this day Vincent,

Holly, Eddie Cochran, and Bill Haley are venerated as British national treasures. (A Buddy Holly CD went to number one on *Music Week*'s pop album chart as recently as 1992, and a stage play about his life has been a box-office smash in London for the past several years.) So, despite a few strident complaints from conservative quarters that the Twist's movements were suggestive and possibly even depraved, the Twist found the same acceptance as rock and roll after it arrived on England's green.

Lionel Blair recalled that during a television workers' strike that halted his TV show, he took the Twist into a triumphant cabaret stage act. "We started with the Charleston, we did the Black Bottom, and then I got everybody up on the floor to do the Twist, and that's how the act ended . . . and so the dance floor was packed." Local stars such as Anthony Newley and visiting American singer Pat Boone attended. The show was so successful in Great Britain that Blair took it on a world tour. "The Twist changed my entire life," he said later.

In 1962, a fledgling record producer named Chris Blackwell pressed up 500 copies of his first ska single, "Twist Baby" by Owen Grey, and sold out on the first day, thus laying the groundwork for his label, Island Records. The enterprise grew from there. A few years later, Blackwell would launch Bob Marley, the Police, and U2 into international stardom.

Across the English Channel, Paris had been in the throes of *"l'affaire Tweest"* since the fall of 1961, and Chez Regine, a chichi discothèque, was packed every night with the City of Lights' most fluorescent luminaries. Chez Regine was owned by Regine Zylberberg, a former employee of the legendary Whiskey à Go Go, who had decorated her nightclub with trees and park benches and hired the very best disc jockeys to spin records for her select clientele. One night the Broadway cast of *West Side Story*, just off the plane from New York, burst into Chez Regine carrying a few of their own recordings. One of the singles was "The Twist" by Chubby Checker. "It's the hottest new dance in New York," they told Regine, and so she gave "The Twist" priority. "Suddenly we became the fashionable nightclub," one of Regine's maître d's told writer Albert Goldman. "People were Twisting everywhere, but it was at Regine's that one could count the most Rothschilds per square meter—and Kennedys and Rockefellers in shirt sleeves." In late October a *New York Times* French correspondent reported: "Until two weeks ago the cha cha and the meringue were as popular here as in the United States. When word reached here that the Twist was the new craze in the United States, almost overnight the sensuous, hip-swiveling dance became the thing to do in Paris."

Along with its ritzy discothèque scene, the city already had a flourishing young black-leather-jacket crowd grooving to a warped form of rockabilly called "yogurt" at such underground clubs as the Golf Drouot; one of the yogurt bands, Dick Rivers et Ses Chats Sauvages (and His Wild Cats), recorded a lively "Twist à Saint Tropez" that became popular. The country's biggest rock and roll star, Johnny Hallyday, a cross between American icons James Dean and Gene Vincent (both of whom were popular in France), got in on the act by recording a Twist album. Another soft rocker, Richard Anthony, recorded a French version of "Let's Twist Again" for France's Columbia. Petula Clark, a former British child star living in Paris in the early 1960s, lit up the French singles charts with "Ya Ya Twist." By early 1962, the sixty-seven-year-old Duke of Windsor was Twisting at a Parisian ball under the tutelage of American fashion model Jackie Ainesworth. "It was amusing," said the former King Edward VIII, who had abdicated the British throne twenty-five years earlier to marry an American commoner, "but a bit strenuous." Actress Audrey Hepburn, after picking up the Twist at Chez Regine, showed her fancy footwork with husband Mel Ferrar aboard the opulent new ocean liner *France*, where her latest film, *Breakfast at Tiffany's*, was having its European premiere. And when a dozen Christian Dior models were flown from Paris to the French embassy in Washington, D.C., for a charity fashion show, the lithe ladies shocked and delighted the diplomatic corps of sev-

eral countries by introducing them to the dance that had originated less than a hundred miles away, in Baltimore.

In Germany, where the Soviets in late 1961 were putting the
finishing touches on their new Berlin Wall, the physical separation of partners dancing the Twist seemed like the perfect art
statement. Chubby Checker arrived singing "Der Twist
Beginnt" ("Let's Twist Again")—recorded in German over the
same instrumental tracks as the English version—but the
cream of West Berlin society at the Eden Saloon Twisted to the
hit record "Liebestraum von Liszt Twist." "This is, this is, this is
the Liebestraum by Liszt, the Liebestraum by Liszt as a Twist,"
went the lyrics (in German, of course), "but nobody can do it
like Lizst; yes, this is, this is, this is the beautiful, world-famous
Liebestraum by Lizst—done as a Twist." Meanwhile, Munich
teenagers danced to the music of Oliver Twist and Die Happy
Twisters in their peppermint-striped skirts with "*Achtung, es
wird getwistet*" (Watch out, we're doing the Twist) embroidered
on the hems. A German doctor publicly warned against "accel-
erating one's hips and legs in opposite directions," and a psy-
chiatrist announced: "The Twist craze can be attributed to
Atomangst"—a kind of free-floating anxiety that Germans were
feeling about being at ground zero of the East-West nuclear
standoff.

In Rome, where Elizabeth Taylor and Richard Burton were
filming the expensive flop *Cleopatra* that would bring the age of
Hollywood's supercolossal costume dramas to an ignoble fiz-
zle, the dozens of dancers flown in from California for the
movie's elaborate dance numbers took time out between scenes
to Twist among the plaster Egyptian columns, to the delight of
paparazzi.

When the rich and playful youth of the Middle East took
the Twist back home from Europe, they were met with steely
disapproval. In Damascus, Syrian Minister of Information
Foudad Adel banned the Twist, branding it "sexually provocative," and ordered that the importation and distribution of all
Twist records be stopped. The Ministry of Culture and National

Guidance in Cairo banned the Twist outright, with no explana-
tion, though that didn't stop Egypt's jet set from Twisting at
posh clubs along the sparkling white beach at Alexandria. And
in Beirut, Interior Minister Kamal Jumblat declared that something must be done about the throngs of young people gyrating
in the Zeitoun nightclub district. Announcing a Twist ban to
"safeguard the morals of Lebanese youth," he sent police to raid
one notorious nightclub. The club manager insisted, uncon-
vincingly, that his patrons were actually doing the tango. At this
point, Justice Minister Fuad Boutros jumped into the fray to
denounce Jumblat's repressive tactics. He wasn't a fan of the
Twist, he said, but he believed in "individual liberty in all its
forms." A Beirut policeman added, "It doesn't seem immoral.
They don't even touch each other."

Not even the Soviet Union was immune to the Twist. While
the U.S. Air Force was installing the final buttons on its underground fleet of silo-bound, nuclear-tipped Minuteman ICBMs
stretching across the Great Plains, rock and roll culture was rat-
tling the Iron Curtain. The Twist took on all the political, social,
and economic ramifications of the Cold War. In Tiflis, Georgia,
not far from Joseph Stalin's birthplace, American soprano
Dorothy Kirsten, in town performing *La Traviata*, did the Twist
at a banquet. When everyone applauded her dips and swivels,
the diva commented to friends, "American culture has triumphed again." Asked if the Twist might sweep Russia, she
said, "As an American—I hope not!"

Meanwhile, in Moscow, Igor Moiseyev, director of Russia's
premier folk-dancing company, deplored "the disgusting dynamism of rock and roll and the Twist" and labeled them
"teddy boy dances" in a jeremiad he delivered to *Izvestia*, the
leading Communist newspaper. "Anyone with healthy tastes is
against their sexual character, their intimacy and their isolation
from everything," he said, adding that American dances
"allow people to forget themselves, which is required apparently by those people who are leading joyless lives." In order
to stop the incursion of decadent Western sashaying like the

Twist, Moiseyev appealed to Soviet choreographers to come up with simple new folk dances that expressed "comradely spirit, kindness and [Russian] dynamism. . . . I am sure that if we have our own everyday dances they will conquer the world in the same way as have our music, songs and ballet." The Soviet government got behind Moiseyev one hundred percent, and over the next couple of years dozens of new Socialist dances such as the Moskvichka, the Terrikon, and even the Slag Heap were introduced. "In keeping with Moiseyev's plan," wrote Timothy Ryback in *Rock Around the Bloc*, a book about Socialist rock music, "the dances were lauded in the press, presented in youth clubs, demonstrated on television. There was just one problem. No one danced them."

Soviet poet Yevgeny Yevtushenko, a man in his twenties who had visited the West and been to a London nightclub, came to the defense of the Twist early in the controversy. "I had heard many stories about the Twist," Yevtushenko wrote in a Moscow literary magazine. "Someone even said it was a typical product of capitalist society. I do not understand how dances can be divided into capitalist and socialist." After praising rock and roll's American working-class origins, he found even more profound beginnings in the so-called 'exotic Twist':

> Couples were dancing in a stuffy, packed hall, filled with cigarette smoke. Bearded youths and girls in tight black trousers wriggled and Twisted. It was not an especially esthetic sight. However, among the Twisters was a young Negro couple dancing with remarkable lightness and grace, white teeth sparkling in the semi-darkness. They danced full of joy, as if they had been used to the dance since childhood. I suddenly realized why they danced the Twist the way they did.
>
> The Twist is advertised as a miracle of the atomic era. But I remembered Ghana jungles two years ago where I watched African tribal dances. Those dances have existed thousands of years. They were ritual dances that had not yet been called the Twist. This miracle of the atomic era is merely a modernized version of what was invented thousands of years ago.

Yevtushenko's acceptance may have been the most realistic approach, but the official party line remained prudishly anti-Twist. The April 6, 1962, issue of *Komsomolskaia Pravda*, the Communist youth paper, tried to stir up fear and loathing of the phenomenon by reporting on its socially destructive effects: "Dozens of cases are known in which possessed dancers of rock 'n' roll and the 'Twist,' the new dance that has come to dominate the variety stages and dance halls of the West, obsessed and infuriated, have demolished the buildings where they were gathered, have broken windows and chairs, and, out in the streets, have staged riots." By the end of the year, Premier Nikita Khrushchev told the Party's Central Committee, "A feeling of distaste is aroused by some of the so-called modern dances brought into our country from the West." And these dances, he emphasized (without having to take off his shoe and pound it on the dais), "are something unseemly, mad, and the devil knows what!"

As one might expect, the repressive rhetoric and the ideological brainwashing had the opposite of their intended effect. In 1964 the newspaper *Vechernyaya Moskva* assessed the results of the use of homegrown dances as a cultural defense against the Twist and other Western dance crazes: "Huge sums have been wasted on authors' honorariums, on the publication of books, notes, records and teaching manuals, on radio and television publicity, programs and on countless seminars." Despite all the propaganda, Russian kids still wanted to Twist. As one correspondent reported that year, "The Twist is being danced privately in homes and small parties, and on Moscow dance floors a couple will occasionally go through a couple of furtive gyrations while no one is looking." The Twist would remain a popular dance among Russian youth throughout much of the 1960s, and as late as May 1967, Moscow police spent an entire night trying to break up a massive spontaneous Twist party in Red Square, under the spires and onion domes of the Kremlin. Perhaps a Russian youth, writing a couple of years earlier to a literary magazine, best summed up the unabated thirst to Twist: "One cannot dance the polonaise in the age of sputniks and computers."

Elsewhere in the Soviet bloc, efficiency experts experimenting with Hungarian textile factory workers discovered that fifteen-minute Twist breaks, where music was played and the employees were allowed to dance, improved efficiency. A scientific board recommended that Communist officials throughout Eastern Europe rethink their policy of treating the Twist as an example of "degenerate Western culture" and implement Twist breaks at other factories. In East Germany, where the Twist had arrived early, in 1961, party ideologues at first denounced it as subversive. At a Communist-sponsored dance forum in Annaberg, the *Sachsische Zeitung* reported, an official "demonstrated that dance music was being used as an instrument of the imperialists in West Germany in order to prepare young people for war." Nonetheless, the following year Horst Schumann, leader of the government-sanctioned Free German Youth movement, reluctantly had to acknowledge that the Twist had become the most popular dance among young German Communists and that the party's efforts to replace it with German dances had failed.

Czechoslovakia, after briefly trying to stamp out the Twist by raiding dance parties, reportedly relented after a nephew of President Antonin Novotny was mistakenly rounded up by police. In Prague the Semafor Theater became home of a Twist and rock and roll musical called *Susan's at Home Alone*. The show became so popular that Supraphone, the state record label, released a soundtrack album that included a bonus song called "The Semafor Twist." The album was a hit throughout the Soviet bloc.

In Poland the Twist launched what would be that country's most significant 1960s rock and roll band, Niebesko Czarni, the first to stress the use of Polish rather than English in rock lyrics and, by extension, to turn rock and roll into more than an unspoken political statement. Niebesko Czarni's earliest Twist recordings were so popular that the group's lead singer, Danuta Skorzynska, was dubbed "Miss Twist."

The Twist even penetrated China's Red Curtain. In late 1962 a Canton newspaper expressed outrage over "ugly displays" of Twisting by young people at Maoming Cultural Park.

But if the footloose, freewheeling Twist was the bane of the rigid Communist world, it represented something equally disruptive and demoralizing to anti-Communists. In a little Indochinese country, the Republic of Vietnam, which most Americans had never heard of and couldn't have cared less about, the Twist was banned because it violated the strict morality laws of Ngo Dinh Diem's Roman Catholic government. President Diem, having previously proscribed the singing of sad songs for fear they might dampen the country's fervency in its struggle against Communism, outlawed not only the Twist itself but the singing of Twist songs. Even the U.S., French, and British embassies in Saigon, the nation's capital, were asked not to play Twist records at their diplomatic parties; the bug might escape the compounds. When one of Saigon's leading newspapers, *Thoi Bao*, criticized the government's Twist prohibition as legally and morally unhealthy, Diem charged the paper with printing articles "degrading and harmful to public decency" and closed it down. But Diem's assault on the Twist was doomed from the start because the Republic of Vietnam hosted several thousand American troops, who listened to Twist recordings daily on the subversive Armed Forces Network.

15: What Are the Kids Doing?

"As it stands I think it's a fad, and a fleeting one.
In two years, it will be forgotten."
—Dr. Albert Ellis, psychologist

Even at the height of its extraordinary popularity, the Twist in America was seen as an aberration, an indulgence, a temporary insanity, a minor sin. It had had its detractors from the very start, but as it spread upward through the country's social echelons all the way to the Camelot in-crowd, so did a creeping backlash against the Twist. In both *Ebony* magazine and the *New York Times*, a Trinidad-born American dancer-choreographer named Geoffrey Holder railed against it as a sign of American crassness, prudery, and social breakdown, all in one fell swoop. "The Twist?" he spat contemptuously.

> I'm sitting this one out. It's dishonest. It's not a dance and it has become dirty. . . . But it's not what it's packaged. It's synthetic sex turned into a sick spectator sport. . . . The oldest hootchy kootchy in the books has become the latest thing. Who would believe it? From the dawn of time, the classic way of showing male potency has been the same pelvic movement. In African fertility dances, you always find it naked, honest.
>
> Other dances have been turned into gimmicks. Here is a gimmick turned into a dance. The Twist happens to be a contortion for children which got taken up by adults. . . . The dances and contortions which pass for dances at any given time tell us something about the society that makes a vogue of them. Decline and fallout frenzy show up on the dance floor.

When former President Dwight Eisenhower returned to his home in Abilene, Kansas, on May 1, 1962, to speak at the dedication of the Eisenhower Library, he took advantage of the assembled press to express his growing concern not over "the unwarranted influence by the military-industrial complex" (which had been the target of his last major speech fifteen months earlier), but rather over the frivolity of modern American life and the attendant slippage of morality. Talking about the sturdy, God-fearing pioneers who settled the West under the most dire conditions, Eisenhower said, "Now I wonder if some of those people could come back today and see us doing the Twist instead of the minuet—whether they would be particularly struck by the beauty of that dance? Now, I have no objection to the Twist, as such, but it does represent some kind of change in our standards." The Twist, according to the ex-president, was just another symptom of the debasement of contemporary art through the use of "vulgarity, sensuality, indeed, downright filth. . . . What has happened to our concept of beauty and decency and morality?" Now that the Twist was a symbol of modern American entertainment, what freakishness did the future hold?

The degeneration of American culture had become a hot topic by the late fifties, brought on in part by the popularity of rock and roll and its victory over established forms of music. In May of 1961, Federal Communications Commission Chairman Newton Minow delivered his famous, much-quoted speech decrying the state of American television: "I invite you to sit down in front of your television set. . . . I can assure you that you will observe a vast wasteland." The analogy, borrowed from T. S. Eliot's apocalyptic poem "The Waste Land," provided a buzzword encompassing all of America's media-driven culture. The Twist became a big chunk of that topography.

As any calm and reasonable critic could have predicted, the Twist would eventually shrivel up and die from its own success and excess, not from any authoritarian reproof or government fiat. A craze has only one form of death: People get tired of it. The ones who first discover and embrace the newest rage abandon it as soon as they see it being taken up by those less hip than themselves, and so it goes, all the way down the hierarchy of hipness, until the fad becomes such an embarrassment to all that a national amnesia sets in and all artifacts are either destroyed or stashed away at the bottom of a trunk in the attic. That would be the fate of the Twist soon enough. And the taint would ruin most of those who had associated their names with it.

Musicologist Robert Pruter saw the first signs of the Twist's downfall in its rise up the social ladder. "Rock and roll from the mid-fifties to about 1966 remained exciting because it was part of a dancehall culture," he said. "The only people who took pride in dancing to rock and roll music and aspired to dancing well were poor and working-class people. The college kids that gave up jazz and folk music in the early sixties and took up rock and roll didn't like dancing. Compare the Madison, which was well choreographed, with the Frug or the Freddie, which didn't even require coordination. Middle-class whites only pantomimed dancing; they had no feel for it. So dance became freeform, and the music lost its excitement because it wasn't dance music anymore." Pruter claimed he first spotted the Twist in early 1960 B.C. (before Chubby), when the black and ethnic kids at his inner-city school started doing it. "They had style, you really enjoyed watching them dance. The Twist didn't get corny until the middle-class white kids started doing it—and then it really got lame after the Twist became a big society thing in 1962 when Jackie Kennedy and Noël Coward were doing it at the Peppermint Lounge."

Overkill and greed also conspired to finish off the Twist. When the Peppermint Lounge charged exorbitant entrance fees at the door and hired a well-choreographed dance troupe in peppermint-striped suits and short skirts to put on revues for tourists, the writing was on more than its bathroom walls: Twist Days Numbered. Uptown, at Smalls' Paradise, Mama Lu Parks's professional team of tasseled black dancers, the Parkettes, officiated over the well-heeled but flat-footed white slummers who'd come for Twist contests, and it was all too slick and ridiculously overpriced to even be called decadent.

What distinguished the Twist from all other dances was the

speed with which it crossed over not just the racial line, but the class and generational lines; it was essentially a black dance appropriated first by white youths and then by their elders. By the summer of 1963, when the Twist had become passé even among adults, writer Allen Hughes delivered a postmortem on the dance in the *New York Times*, in which he expressed his happiness that "exhausted oldsters have come to realize that it was never right for them." Hughes considered the Twist "a thoroughly natural, serviceable and decent impetus for the release of pent-up physical and emotional energy" for young people. It only became obscene when their parents took up the dance. "The Twist was revolting then because the wrong people were doing it, and doing it for the wrong reasons. They were also watching it, or, rather, leering at it, and again for the wrong reasons." Unable to account "for the wholesale lapse of taste and common sense on the part of adults," Hughes hoped that as young people devised new dances, "the old will . . . stay out of the way. And, hopefully, the old will be a bit more sensible in the future . . . about trying to adopt dance styles unsuited to them."

16: The Twist Will Never Die

> "I wonder if any M.P. would care to sponsor a private members bill outlawing the return of the Twist."
> –the *London Evening Standard*, 1988

In 1962, the National Academy of Recording Arts and Sciences (NARAS) added the category of Best Rock and Roll Recording to its Grammy Awards in time for the 1961 season. The Academy, even squarer then than it is now, put together a panel of middle-of-the-road rock producers—Lou Adler, Nick Venet, and Jimmie Haskell—to help sort out a list of nominees. "[Bandleader] Paul Weston and [singer] Margaret Whiting came to me and said they wanted someone to represent the music that was happening at the time," Adler told writer Henry Schipper. "It was very, very frustrating. They didn't relate to, understand, or accept the music. They thought the songs were nonsense."

Chubby Checker's "Let's Twist Again" won the first Best Rock and Roll Recording Grammy, beating out James Darren's "Goodbye Cruel World," Chris Kenner's "I Like It Like That," Ike and Tina Turner's "It's Gonna Work Out Fine," and the Tokens's "The Lion Sleeps Tonight." Despite the popularity of Checker's version of "The Twist" at the beginning of the following year, it didn't qualify because it had been released first in 1960, before there was a Grammy for rock and roll. Sam Cooke's "Twistin' the Night Away" was nominated for Best Rock and Roll Recording in 1962, but it lost to Danish instrumentalist Bent Fabric's ultracool but hardly rocking "Alley Cat."

After the modest financial success of *Hey, Let's Twist*, Harry Romm rushed a second Joey Dee film into production in the spring of 1962 but moved the action from the Peppermint

Lounge to Paris, where the Twist was still hot. The film's working title was *Viva La Twist*, but by the time it came out, the Twist had cooled off and Paramount, not wanting to sink with a fading fad or be stuck with an unintentionally ironic title, released the movie as *Two Tickets to Paris*.

Joey Dee and the Starliters's success as a down 'n' dirty white rhythm and blues group spawned countless imitators, but their influence on at least two groups was direct. By 1964 the Starliters consisted of David Brigati's younger brother Eddie, a Canadian guitarist named Gene Cornish, and New York keyboardist Felix Cavaliere. When these three members broke away from Joey Dee the following year and joined forces with jazz drummer Dino Danelli, they carried on the Starliters's danceable, organ-based, blue-eyed soul sound under the name the Young Rascals and became one of the latter-sixties' steadiest hitmakers.

A second group got its first major exposure as part of Joey Dee and the Starliters's stage act. As soon as the Peppermint Lounge became the hottest place in Manhattan in early October 1961, sisters Veronica and Estelle Bennett and their cousin Nedra Talley, who sang as a rock and roll trio called Ronnie and the Relatives, decided that they should go where the action was even though two of them were still in high school. The three Spanish Harlem girls padded their bras, applied liberal amounts of makeup, teased their hair a foot high, and squeezed themselves into provocative dresses in hopes of fooling the club's doorman. While they were standing in line, said Veronica, the doorman brought the manager out. "As soon as he saw us he said, 'What are you doing out here on line? You're already late.' . . . It didn't take us long to figure out that he'd hired a girl group to dance at the club, but they obviously hadn't shown up, so he assumed *we* were them."

The club was jammed as they worked their way to the stage where Joey Dee and the Starliters were playing. After the girls began dancing, one of the Starliters handed Veronica the microphone during a rave-up Ray Charles song—"almost as a prank," she said. "But holding a mike was no joke to me. I grabbed it from his hands and tore through a version of 'What'd I Say?' that brought the house down." The manager hired the girls during intermission as the club's official go-go dancers and part-time singers.

When Columbia Pictures came to the Peppermint to film *Hey, Let's Twist*, the Starliters wanted the trio to play their girl-friends in the film. But the girls, part black, part Puerto Rican, didn't have the right complexions. The director told Dee, "We can't use them. They're too light to play black girls and too dark to play white girls. The audience wouldn't know if they were supposed to be white or black." Veronica, her sister, and her cousin had to be content to play dancers in a crowd scene. And when the film opened, "We were probably the only girls in New York who cried all the way through *Hey, Let's Twist*." They would have to wait another year or so before they became the Ronettes, easily the most distinctive-sounding girl group of the 1960s, under the auspices of record producer Phil Spector.

By October 1962 the Twist was gone from the British charts — the editors of the *New Oxford English Dictionary* only the previous month had decided not to include "Twist" in their newest edition because the dance hadn't yet stood "the test of time"— but 1963 brought back lingering echoes. Pretty, bouffant-haired singer Helen Shapiro, Columbia Records's teenage star of the film *It's Trad Dad!*, encored in a trifle called *Play It Cool*, co-starring British soft-rocker Billy Fury and American pop singer Bobby Vee. "Twist vs. Swing!" shouted the ad line beneath the title on the movie poster. "International Twisters and World-famed Swingers crash head-on in musical, dancing battle royal!"

Perhaps more enduring was a remake of the Isley Brothers's hit "Twist and Shout" by the Beatles, recorded during a marathon February 11, 1963, Abbey Road Studios session at which they recorded thirteen songs for their first album, *Please Please Me*. Their producer, George Martin, recalled in his memoirs: "All we did really was to reproduce the Cavern performances in the comparative calm of the studio. I say 'comparative' because there was one number which always caused a furore in the Cavern — 'Twist and Shout.' John [Lennon] absolutely screamed it. God alone knows what he did to his larynx each time he performed it, because he made a sound rather like tearing flesh. That *had* to be right on the first take, because I knew perfectly well that if we had to do it a second time it would never be as good." EMI released "Twist and Shout" and three other songs on the Beatles's first EP, and the record shot to number one on the British singles chart. (A cover recording by Brian Poole and the Tremeloes reached number four.) But as a Twist record, "Twist and Shout" was an anomaly, and an ironic one at that, for the arrival of the Beatles on Britain's pop charts in early 1963 had effectively rendered the Twist as passé as the Twist had made trad jazz less than two years earlier. Besides, anyone who ever tried to Twist to the Beatles' "Twist and Shout" knows that it doesn't have a very good Twist rhythm. Still, the Brits could never get the Twist completely out of their system. In 1975 the Twist resurfaced when British vocalist John Asher recorded a hit remake of "Let's Twist Again," and London Records covered it by reissuing Chubby Checker's "Let's Twist Again" — backed with "The Twist." Chubby's single rose to number five on the *Music Week* pop chart, its fifth entry since 1961. In 1983 the Twist returned again, accompanied by a couple of new hit recordings by Chill Fac-Tor ("Twist [Round 'N' Round]") and Dire Straits ("Twisting by the Pool"), and, five years later, in 1988, both Chubby Checker (teaming with rappers the Fat Boys on a new version of "The Twist") and the American all-girl group Salt 'N' Pepa ("Twist and Shout") put Twist singles on the British charts.

In the latter half of 1962, after American youth had moved on to other variations on the Twist, as well as surf music, the adults floundered. The Bossa Nova, a Brazilian dance with a catchy rhythm, became a brief substitute, but as Ralph Mitchell, owner of the Scene in Chicago, put it, "[The Bossa Nova's] not as primitive as the Twist. You can't fake it as well." The Fred Astaire Dance Studios promoted the idea of "doing the Twist to bossa nova rhythm, which comes out like a mambo," but it was nonsense. Latin rhythms and dances come and go as novelties in the U.S., but so far they have never been very popular with white teenagers, possibly because they are not organic to American music.

The Arthur Murray and Fred Astaire studio chains, having so crassly exploited the Twist, stumbled during the dance's decline, ruined by the flush of success. The California state attorney general charged the studios—autonomous franchises that paid 10 to 15 percent of their profits to the Murray and Astaire headquarters in New York—with racketeering. The studios' high-pressure salesmen and promotional schemes had induced dance students to sign contracts for "lifetime" courses for up to $10,000, far in excess of what California law allowed.

On April 12, 1964, at a Lutheran church in Pennsauken, New Jersey, Chubby Checker married Catherina Lodders, a twenty-two-year-old Dutch model who had won the title of Miss World a year earlier. The mixed marriage—the *New York Times* pointedly referred to Checker as a "Negro rock 'n' roll singer" and remarked that the minister "made no reference to the interracial nature of the marriage"—came during an increasingly tense period in this country's racial politics, and yet it never raised the hackles as did, say, Sammy Davis Jr.'s marriage to Swedish actress Mae Britt during that same era.

Chubby Checker spent the early sixties cranking out dance hits until his regular chart visitations ended in 1965. His last charter in the 1960s came at the end of the decade, after he had left Parkway and gone to Buddah Records. His version of the Beatles's "Back in the U.S.S.R." was a small hit. Thirteen years later he returned to the bottom of the charts when he signed with MCA and recorded a song called "Running." But it would be "The Twist" itself that eventually returned him to the American Top Forty.

In 1988 Chubby teamed up with his modern-day heavyweight counterparts, a rap trio called the Fat Boys, to remake

"The Twist" as "The Twist (Yo, Twist!)" on the Tin Pan Apple label (887571). Modern dance music had doubled back on the original hit record that spawned it. The Fat Boys were a novelty act out of Brooklyn. Prince Markie Dee (Mark Morales) and Kool Rock (Damon Wimbley) rapped while the heaviest of the three, the Human Beat Box (Darren Robinson), supplied the rhythm with an amazing range of vocal sounds. Discovered at a talent contest at Manhattan's Radio City Music Hall, the three began recording as the Disco 3 in 1984 for Sutra Records, a Mafia-connected label owned by Morris Levy and Olympia Esposito, the longtime mistress of Genovese godfather Vincent Gigante. When the rappers' first record, "Fat Boys," became an R & B hit, they changed their name to the Fat Boys. After a half-dozen local hits and an appearance in a popular rap film called *Krush Groove*, their management created Tin Pan Apple Records as their new label and signed a marketing and distribution deal with Polygram Records.

In 1986 a Bronx rap group named Run-D.M.C. invented a new hybrid of rock and roll hip-hop when it teamed up with members of the heavy metal rock group Aerosmith to record a rap version of a 1977 Aerosmith hit called "Walk This Way." The remake, bolstered by a popular video that got maximum "rotation" on MTV, walked that way up to number four on the pop charts and exposed a new segment of mainstream white record buyers to rap. (Although it had become a viable industry in 1980 when the Sugarhill Gang had a modest hit with "Rapper's Delight," rap was still largely a ghetto music in 1986.) The Fat Boys dove into this rock 'n' rap smorgasbord by joining up with the Beach Boys to record a hip-hop version of a 1963 surf hit by the Surfaris called "Wipeout" (which essentially was a rip-off of a 1959 record called "Bongo Rock" by black percussionist Preston Epps). The single not only put the Fat Boys on the pop charts for the first time in their three-year recording career, it reached as high as number twelve. And since nothing succeeds like excess, the trio rubbed their big, hanging tummies and looked around for another oldie that they could record with an original artist. Their hungry eyes fell upon "The Twist"—and Chubby Checker.

The result was "The Twist (Yo, Twist!)" by the Fat Boys "with stupid def vocals by Chubby Checker." The performance was broken into alternating choruses of Chubby singing "The Twist" as he had sung it in 1960, and the Fat Boys rapping about putting together a Twist party. Checker's half of the record suffered in the comparison. Most of his musical and rhythmic background was provided by Mac Quayle's keyboards, overdubbed on top of each other. To most people raised on nonelectronic music (i.e., those familiar with Checker's original single), the synthesizer sounds tinny and toylike. However, the young record buyers who determine what goes into the Top Forty consider the synthesizer a valid musical instrument. For them, "The Twist (Yo, Twist!)" made the Twist new again, at least for a few weeks. The record reached number sixteen.

Cameo-Parkway suffered its greatest loss when patron Dick Clark defected from Philly to Los Angeles in March 1964. By then, Kal Mann had already retired (in 1963), and Dave Appell had moved on to other projects. Bernie Lowe sold the company to a couple of Texas businessmen a year or two later. In July 1967, Allen Klein, the manager of the Rolling Stones and several other heavy-duty British rock acts, bought controlling interest in Cameo-Parkway and made himself many millions of dollars in paper profits when the company stock rocketed from four dollars to over seventy-six dollars a share. Endlessly wheeling and dealing his way through boardrooms and courtrooms, during which time the American Stock Exchange halted trading of the company stock, Klein merged Cameo-Parkway with his accounting company to form ABKCO Industries, a rock management conglomerate that over the next few years would drive the costs of making records with major acts into the stratosphere and turn rock music into the corporate commodity it is today. Rumors that Klein had illegally inflated the worth of Cameo-Parkway's stock just before the merger brought the Securities and Exchange Commission into the picture, but no charges were ever filed. ABKCO still owns the Cameo-Parkway masters and has made no apparent effort to reissue them.

The Twist went on and on, of course, under other names and with variations added to or subtracted from it. America through most of the 1960s was, in the words of Cannibal and the Headhunters, the "Land of 1000 Dances": the Pony, the Loco-Motion, the Frug, the Fly, the Mashed Potatoes, the Bugaloo, the Jerk, the Monkey (a faster Jerk), the Hitchhike, the Swim. They were all wild, formless pantomimes and mimickry that let people express themselves kinetically, but essentially they remained the Twist with double headlights, bigger tailfins, and overdrive. The Twist started the trend. Whites could now dance not only with their feet but with their hips and who knows what else? All the gyrations that followed were simply attempts to recapture the magic of the Twist.

Along with this dance fever came a new American institution, the discotheque. The Peppermint Lounge's dancing waitresses, shaking their booty on the club's wrought-iron railings, became the world's first go-go dancers, and by January 1965, when the British Invasion had taken over the discotheque scene, Los Angeles club owner Elmer Valentine brought the Whiskey A-Go-Go to America, or, more specifically, to West Hollywood's Sunset Strip, and furnished it with cages above the stage in which scantily clad girls could shake and shimmy in their miniskirts and white "go-go boots."

In 1965 five thousand discotheques opened throughout the United States as seemingly palsied Americans went gaga over go-go. None other than Chubby Checker introduced the term to record buyers in "At the Discotheque," the flipside of one of his minor dance hits, "Do the Freddie." (A year later the Miracles shimmied onto the record charts with "Going to a Go-Go.") From September 1964 to early 1966, the beautiful and lithe Shindig Dancers, decked out in tight, fringed skirts and boots, carried on the permutations of the Twist on ABC-TV's highly rated "Shindig" program, as top recording artists from the Rolling Stones to Sonny and Cher rocked out. On NBC's "Hullabaloo," such rock and roll stars as the Dave Clark Five and the Ronettes were accompanied by the hip-quaking Hullabaloo Dancers, including Miss Lada Edmund Jr., known as "the girl in the cage," who spent over a year seriously Frugging and hair-tossing above the crowd. In its zeal to create the atmosphere of a discotheque going full blast, the show even called one segment Hullabaloo A-Go-Go. At the same time, independent television stations ran a syndicated rock and roll program called "Hollywood A-Go-Go," populated, once again, with dancing girls in tight sweaters and go-go boots.

There are several links between the Twist and the excesses of the late-seventies disco era, beyond the obvious mutation of one dance into another. Equally important is the connection between the dance recordings of Parkway in the sixties and of Casablanca Records more than ten years later—in the person and symbol of Neil Bogart, Casablanca's founder. Raised in Brooklyn, Bogart briefly recorded in the early sixties as an adenoidal teen fop, then moved into record promotion. He joined Cameo-Parkway in 1967 as vice president and sales manager. When Allen Klein took over the company, Bogart jumped ship along with several fellow employees (and Chubby Checker) and became general manager of a new record label called Buddah, a Mafia front operation (mobster Sonny Franzese was a silent partner) run by several young music hustlers willing to do anything for a buck.

Driven by the same contempt for music and the youth marketplace that Cameo-Parkway had been, the Buddah boys gave the world a new, studio-manufactured, hype-driven genre: bubblegum music. Buddah's hit-making artists, the Ohio Express and the 1910 Fruitgum Company, did not exist outside the studio. And thus Bogart took to heart Cameo-Parkway's greatest lesson: Modern music is a producer's medium, with mostly interchangeable and expendable artists, supported by excessive promotion. To Bogart, music was nothing more than a monotonous procession of gimmicks, trends, and fads—a rhythmic drone; the more anonymous the better—and the job of the record company was either to spot them coming and flog them into a mania, or else create them out of whole cloth and pure hype. When Neil Bogart, fueled by neon dreams and a steady diet of cocaine, launched his own Casablanca label in the mid-1970s and gave the world Donna Summer and the Village People, not to mention the *Night at Studio 54* album and the *Flashdance* soundtrack, the destructive legacy of Cameo-Parkway (and more indirectly the Twist) was complete.

And finally, back where it began, there was Hank Ballard. Though his original recording of "The Twist" had been greatly overshadowed by Checker's hit, he believes its banishment from "American Bandstand" in favor of the cover version provided him with a bargaining chip with Dick Clark, who heavily promoted both "Finger Poppin' Time" (number seven) and "Let's Go, Let's Go, Let's Go" (number six) in 1960. The following year, with Dick Clark's help, four Ballard singles—"The Hoochi Coochi Coo," "Let's Go Again (Where We Went Last Night)," "The Continental Walk," and "The Switch-A-Roo"—went into the Top Forty and cashed in on the craze of line dances and gyrations inspired by Chubby Checker's string of records. But Ballard was unable to fully capitalize on the second rise of "The Twist" in late 1961 and early 1962. His later Twist recordings—"Miss Twister," "It's Twistin' Time," and "Good Twistin' Tonight"—were mostly album filler. His later re-recording of "The Twist," done without the Midnighters in 1968, was never released.

Cal Green missed the full flush of "The Twist" altogether. "They busted me for possession down in Texas in 1959, and I kinda sat the whole thing out. That's why I wasn't in a position to fight for my credit as songwriter." By the time he returned to the Midnighters in 1962, the Twist craze had ended.

The Midnighters broke up in 1965. "Some of the guys became Black Muslims, they didn't want to perform for white people anymore because the white man was the devil," Ballard said. "I couldn't deal with that. So I broke with them and went to court to keep the Midnighters name. It was tough on me because they were the act, they're the ones that did everything on stage. Me, I just sang." King Records finally dropped him in 1969. Ballard recorded briefly for Chess, Polydor, and Sugar Hill (another label tainted by Morris Levy's involvement and Mob money) but his recording career was largely over.

Today Ballard seems to be in great physical and mental shape. Since coming out of retirement and reforming a new group of Midnighters in 1982, he has been touring the world and, on rare occasions, recording. He denies feeling bitter about being upstaged by Chubby Checker. "If Chubby hadn't recorded it, it wouldn't have been as big as it was." Still, in 1990, when Chubby Checker appeared as the "creator of the Twist" in a TV commercial for Oreo cookies, Ballard's legal representatives demanded that the advertising agency either change the wording or pull the commercial off the air altogether. The agency softened Checker's claim.

For many years Hank Ballard didn't fully benefit from being the guy below the title. He fell on bad times and let the songwriter rights to "The Twist" get away from him. In a couple of vaguely worded 1975 documents, he sold his composer rights to "The Twist" and some other songs for $5,000, and covered a $25,000 loan by signing over his BMI performance rights. The recipient in both cases was Morris Levy, whose Big Seven publishing company already owned Joey Dee's "Peppermint Twist" (Levy owned nearly every song ever released on Roulette Records). But, luckily for Ballard, "The Twist" was subject to the federal copyright act that had been in effect before January 1, 1978: Songs were protected for twenty-eight years and then lapsed into the public domain unless the copyright was renewed for another twenty-eight years. In cases of conflicting renewal claims, the law generally favors the composer. When Ballard joined forces with Chuck Rubin, who heads up a Manhattan firm called Artists Rights Enforcement Corporation, Rubin and his attorneys discovered that the demo of "The

Twist," with its different lyrics, had been protected by an earlier, August 1, 1958, copyright originally held by Gladstone Music, that preceded the January 5, 1959, copyright held by King Records's publishing arms, Jay & Cee Music and Armo Music. Artists Rights took on veteran publisher Fred Bienstock, whose Fort Knox Music controls the song's publishing along with Trio Music in Los Angeles. "It's very complicated," Rubin says guardedly, "We've got certain rights back, but there's still a level of frustration over certain aspects. Our claim is in limbo. We did get back the BMI rights." Now when Ballard boasts, "I gave the world the biggest dance craze ever," he can add that to some extent he's also getting paid for it.

Allen Klein, the owner of the Cameo-Parkway catalog, has not reissued Chubby Checker's music on CD. It's probably just as well, because the other Cameo-Parkway material that he has released is generally inferior. For example, he mastered a Dovells greatest hits CD from vinyl records, not from the original tapes. ("Allen doesn't care," is how Jerry Gross of the Dovells put it.) However, a German Chubby Checker album, *Der Twist Beginnt* (Bear Family 15339), is available—if you'd like to hear Chubby sing a few songs *auf Deutsch*. "The Twist (Yo, Twist!)" is available on the Fat Boys's *Coming Back Hard Again* CD (Polydor/Tin Pan Apple 835 809-2). Hank Ballard's early 1958 demo of "The Twist" can be found on *A Taste of Doo-Wop—Volume 1* (Vee-Jay NVD2-709), and his unadulterated November 1958 King Records master of "The Twist" is on Rhino Records's *Sexy Ways: The Best of Hank Ballard & the Midnighters* CD (R2 71512). Rhino has also released *Hey, Let's Twist: The Best of Joey Dee & the Starliters* (R2 70965).

In 1993 an affectionate, fast-paced seventy-eight-minute documentary film called *Twist* by Canadian filmmaker Ron Mann, blending old photographs and film clips with new interviews, opened briefly at selected theaters around North America and was televised on Great Britain's Channel Four. "It took three days to shoot and three years to edit, yet another year to release . . . so, I'm twisted out, you might say," Mann said in

1994. He had searched through four hundred hours of stock footage, surveyed three thousand songs including some three hundred Twist numbers, scanned over a thousand photographs, watched all the fifties rock 'n' roll movies, and finally filmed his own interviews with Hank Ballard, Chubby Checker, Joey Dee, Dee Dee Sharp, Cholly Atkins, and several middle-aged, former "regulars" from "American Bandstand"'s Philadelphia days. "This is the real story of dirty dancing," Mann said. *Twist* is available on both videocassette (New Line) and Laserdisc (Voyager), and anyone who has enjoyed reading this book will love it.

Fast forward to March 17, 1994, St. Patrick's Day at the Tam O'Shanter, an old Scottish pub in Los Angeles, where a rocking, packed-house party of green-clad revelers was in progress. When boogie woogie pianist Bobby "Fats" Mizzell, a veteran of the Big Bopper's band of thirty-six years earlier, suddenly broke into a seamless medley of "The Twist" and "Let's Twist Again," everybody, young and old and in-between, started Twisting like crazy. At the center of the happy, writhing mob was a particularly attractive young brunette in tight black slacks who had obviously been born in the early 1970s, ten years after the Twist, but she was Twisting with the ease and fluidity of someone for whom the movements were second nature. Afterward, I playfully asked her, "Hey, is the Twist coming back?" Her eyes flashed disapprovingly and her nose rose a few inches. "I never knew it went away," she said.

Appendix A

The Fourteen Most Well-Known Versions
of "The Twist"

1. Hank Ballard and the Midnighters, 1959; overdubbed 1960
2. Chubby Checker, 1960
3. Little Sisters, 1961 (used same instrumental track as Checker's record)
4. King Curtis, 1961 (recorded live at Smalls' Paradise club in Harlem)
6. King Curtis, 1961 (studio recording)
6. Joey Dee and the Starliters, 1962
6. Ronettes (included on a 1963 Crystals album called
   The Crystals Sing the Greatest Hits)
7. Ernie Freeman (charted in the Hot 100 in 1962)
8. Danny Peppermint, 1962
9. The Olympics, 1962
10. Sam Cooke, 1962
11. Duane Eddy, 1962
12. The Champs, 1962
13. Ray Anthony, 1962
14. The Fat Boys with Chubby Checker, 1988

Appendix B

The Twenty-three Twist Records
That Made the American Top Forty

Tabulated by *Billboard*

Chart
position

   #1 — "The Twist" (1960) by Chubby Checker

   #1 — "The Twist" (1962) by Chubby Checker

   #1 — "Peppermint Twist—Part 1" (1962) by Joey Dee and the Starliters

   #2 — "Twist and Shout" (1964) by the Beatles

   #3 — "Slow Twistin' " (1962) by Chubby Checker (with Dee Dee Sharp)

   #8 — "Let's Twist Again" (1961) by Chubby Checker

   #9 — "Dear Lady Twist" (1962) by Gary "U.S." Bonds

   #9 — "Twist, Twist Senora" (1962) by Gary "U.S." Bonds

   #9 — "Twistin' the Night Away" (1962) by Sam Cooke

  #10 — "Percolator (Twist)" (1962) by Billy Joe and the Checkmates

  #12 — "Dancin' Party" (1962) by Chubby Checker (refers to Twistin' party)

  #16 — "The Twist" (1988) by the Fat Boys with Chubby Checker

  #17 — "Soul Twist" (1962) by King Curtis and His Noble Knights

  #17 — "Twist and Shout" (1962) by the Isley Brothers

  #20 — "Hey, Let's Twist" (1962) by Joey Dee and the Starliters

  #22 — "Twistin' Matilda" (1962) by Jimmy Soul

  #25 — "Twist It Up" (1963) by Chubby Checker

  #26 — "Twist-Her" (1962) by Bill Black's Combo

  #27 — "Bristol Twistin' Annie" (1962) by the Dovells

  #27 — "Twistin' U.S.A." (1960) by Danny and the Juniors

  #28 — "The Twist" (1960) by Hank Ballard and the Midnighters

  #34 — "Twistin' Postman" (1962) by the Marvelettes

  #40 — "The Alvin Twist" (1962) by the Chipmunks

Appendix C

*The Twenty-three Twist Hits on the
United Kingdom's Top Fifty*

Tabulated by *Record Retailer* (before 1969) and British Market Research
Bureau/Guinness

Chart
position

#2——"Let's Twist Again" (1961) by Chubby Checker

#2——"The Twist" (1988) by the Fat Boys with Chubby Checker

#4——"Twist and Shout" (1963) by Brian Poole and the Tremeloes

#4——"Twist and Shout" (1988) by Salt 'N' Pepa

#5——"Let's Twist Again"/"The Twist" (1975) by Chubby Checker

#6——"Twistin' the Night Away" (1962) by Sam Cooke

#14——"The Twist" (1962) by Chubby Checker

#14——"Ya Ya Twist" (1962) by Petula Clark

#14——"Let's Twist Again" (1975) by John Asher

#14——"Twisting by the Pool" (1983) by Dire Straits

#19——"Dancin' Party" (1962) by Chubby Checker

#22——"Don't Stop Twist" (1962) by Frankie Vaughan

#22——"Everybody's Twisting" (1962) by Frank Sinatra

#23——"Slow Twistin' " (1962) by Chubby Checker

#26——"The Peppermint Twist" (1962) by Danny Peppermint and the
          Jumping Jacks

#33——"Peppermint Twist" (1962) by Joey Dee and the Starliters

#37——"Twist (Round 'N' Round)" (1983) by Chill Fac-Tor

#42——"Twist and Shout" (1963) by the Isley Brothers

#44——"The Twist" (1960) by Chubby Checker

#45——"Teach Me to Twist" (1960) by Chubby Checker and Bobby Rydell

#46——"Let's Twist Again" (1962) by Chubby Checker

#47——"Twistin' the Night Away" (1985) by Divine

#48——"Twist Twist" (1962) by Chakachas

Update

DAVE APPELL is retired from the music business. He lives between Cherry Hill, New Jersey, and his winter home in Pompano Beach, Florida.

HANK BALLARD lives in Los Alamitos, California, south of Los Angeles. He tours and records with a new group of Midnighters. His Cadillac's license plate reads: TWISTR.

BERNIE BENNICK died in Philadelphia in 1993.

BILL BLACK died of a brain tumor in 1965.

GARY "U.S." BONDS renewed his recording career in 1981 when Bruce Springsteen produced an album for him. One of the singles from the LP, "This Little Girl," rose to number eleven on the pop charts. Bonds continues to perform.

FREDDY CANNON lives in Tarzana, California, and remains a top draw on the oldies circuit.

CHUBBY CHECKER lives on Philadelphia's famed Main Line— known for its picturesque mansions. He performs regularly on the road. In 1994 he recorded a boot-scootin' country album in Nashville.

DICK CLARK is the president of one of television's most prolific production companies, Dick Clark Productions, in Burbank, California. He is among America's richest men.

JOE COOK lives in Revere, Massachusetts, and remains active on the oldies and nightclub circuit.

SAM COOKE was shot to death in Los Angeles in late 1964.

BUDDY DEANE is retired and lives in Little Rock, Arkansas.

JOEY DEE lives in Seminole, Florida, where he is the president emeritus of the National Music Foundation, which maintains a sixty-three-acre retirement facility in Massachusetts for aging and infirm music artists.

ERNIE FREEMAN died in Hawaii in 1981.

HENRY GLOVER died in New York City in 1991.

CHARLIE GRACIE lives in Havertown, Pennsylvania, and continues to perform, mostly in Europe.

CAL GREEN lives between Los Angeles and Texas.

FRANK GUIDA retired from record producing in the mid-1980s, and now lives in the Norfolk area.

RENE HALL died in Los Angeles in 1986.

THE ISLEY BROTHERS recorded over sixty R & B hits from 1962 to the late 1980s, and they continue to perform. (Brothers Ernie and Marvin Isley and cousin Chris Jaspar joined the group in the early 1970s.) O'Kelly Isley died in 1986.

SAM KATZMAN died in 1973.

KING CURTIS was stabbed to death while trying to break up an altercation in Harlem in 1971.

MORRIS LEVY was convicted of two counts of extortion conspiracy in 1988, but died of cancer in 1990 before he could begin serving his prison sentence.

BERNIE LOWE died in 1993, after being inducted into the Philadelphia Walk of Fame.

TONY MAMARELLA died in the 1970s.

KAL MANN is retired and lives in Pompano Beach, Florida.

JOHN MEDORA lives in Los Angeles and is still involved in the music publishing and production business.

SYD NATHAN died in Miami Beach in 1968.

BOBBY ROBINSON lives in New York City and continues to work with new artists.

BROTHER JOE WALLACE lives in Durham, North Carolina, and tours extensively on the gospel circuit with the Sensational Nightingales.

DAVE WHITE lives in Orange County, California, and is trying to produce a film based on his experiences with Danny and the Juniors.

Sources

Books

Bronson, Fred. *The Billboard Book of Number One Hits*. New York: Billboard Publications, 1985.

Brown, James, with Bruce Tucker. *James Brown: The Godfather of Soul*. New York: Macmillan, 1986.

Buckman, Peter. *Let's Dance*. New York: Paddington Press, 1978.

Carpozi, George, Jr. *Let's Twist*. New York: Pyramid Books, 1962.

Clark, Dick, and Richard Robinson. *Rock, Roll and Remember*. New York: Thomas Y. Crowell Co., 1976.

Dannen, Fredric. *Hit Men*. New York: Times Books, 1990.

Dawson, Jim, and Steve Propes. *What Was the First Rock 'n' Roll Record?* Boston: Faber and Faber, 1992.

Eliot, Marc. *Rockonomics*. New York: Citadel Press, 1993.

Gillett, Charlie. *The Sound of the City*. New York: Pantheon Books, 1983.

Goldman, Albert. *Disco*. New York: Hawthorn Books, 1978.

Haley, Alex, and Malcolm X. *The Autobiography of Malcolm X*. New York: Ballantine, 1973.

Jackson, John A. *Big Beat Heat*. New York: Schirmer Books, 1991.

Jasen, David A. *Tin Pan Alley*. New York: Donald I. Fine, 1988.

Jonas, Gerald. *Dancing*. New York: Harry N. Abrams, 1992.

Jones, Wayne. *Rockin', Rollin' & Rappin'*. Frasier, MI: Goldmine Press, 1980.

McCarthy, Todd, and Charles Flynn, ed. *Kings of the Bs*. New York: E. P. Dutton 1975.

Nathan, Hans. *Dan Emmett and the Rise of Early Negro Minstrelsy*. Norman, Okla: University of Oklahoma Press, 1962.

Picardie, Justine, and Dorothy Wade. *Music Man*. New York: W. W. Norton, 1990.

Ribowsky, Mark. *He's a Rebel*. New York: E. P. Dutton, 1989.

Rice, Jo and Tim Rice. *The Guinness Book of British Hit Singles, 1952–1977*. London: Guinness Superlatives, 1977.

Ryback, Timothy W. *Rock Around the Bloc*. Oxford: Oxford University Press, 1990.

Schipper, Henry. *Broken Record*. New York: Birch Lane Press, 1992.

Shaw, Arnold. *Black Popular Music in America*. New York: Schirmer Books, 1986.

Shaw, Arnold. *Honkers and Shouters*. New York: Collier Books, 1978.

Shore, Michael, with Dick Clark. *The History of American Bandstand*. New York: Ballantine Books, 1985.

Smith, Joe. *Off the Record*. New York: Warner Books, 1988.

Smith, Wes. *The Pied Pipers of Rock 'n' Roll*. Marietta, Ga: Longstreet Press, 1989.

Spector, Ronnie, with Vince Waldron. *Be My Baby*. New York: Harmony Books, 1990.

Stearns, Marshall, and Jean Stearns. *Jazz Dance*. New York: Schirmer Books, 1968.

Tracy, Steven C. *Going to Cincinnati*. Chicago: University of Illinois Press, 1993.

Whitburn, Joel. *Top R&B Singles 1942–1988*. Menomonee Falls, Wi: Record Research, 1988.

———. *The Billboard Book of Top 40 Hits*. New York: Billboard Publications, 1985.

Articles

Alden, Robert. "French Dancers Import the Twist." *New York Times*, October 29, 1961.

"American Twist . . . or Twisted Americans." *Senior Scholastic*, January 10, 1962.

"And Now Everybody Is Doing It, the Twist." *Life*, November 24, 1961.

Barber, Rowland. "The Seven Days of Sam Katzman." *Show*, June 1962.

"Bossa Nova, The." *Newsweek*, November 26, 1962.

Burke, Tony, and Dave Penny. "Hank Ballard Interview." *Blues & Rhythm: The Gospel Truth*, Issue 26, January–February 1987.

"Cafe Society Rediscovers Harlem." *Ebony*, June 1962.

Checker, Chubby, and Geoffrey Holder. "To Twist or Not to Twist," *Ebony*, February 1962.

"Chubby Checker Sparks Twist Craze." *Ebony*, January 1961.

Coleman, Rick. "Hank Takes Annie to the Jazz Fest." *Wavelength*, May 1987.

"Dancing Studios Face Coast Study." *New York Times*, October 1, 1962.

Dannen, Fredric. "The Godfather of Rock & Roll." *Rolling Stone*, November 17, 1988.

Dawson, Jim. "Hank Ballard: 'Work with Me, Annie'." *Rip*, June 1987.

———. "The Twist." *Goldmine*, December 16, 1988.

"Der Liszt Twist." *Time*, February 16, 1962.

"Fat For Fun and Profit." *Ebony*, February 1988.

Fishwick, Marshall. "The Twist: Brave New Whirl." *Saturday Review*, March 3, 1962.

"Good Turn." *Newsweek*, February 5, 1962.

Gelb, Arthur. "Habitues of Meyer Davis Land Dance the Twist." *New York Times*, October 19, 1961.

Grendysa, Peter. "King/Federal." *Goldmine*, September 7, 1990.

Holder, Geoffrey. "The Twist? It's Not a Dance." *New York Times Magazine*, December 3, 1961.

Hopkins, Jerry. "Hula City." *Los Angeles Times Magazine: Traveling in Style*, October 17, 1993.

Hughes, Allen. "Though the Fad Is Gone, Twisting Lives On." *New York Times*, July 28, 1963.

Hunt, Dennis. "'The Twist' and Turns of Ballard's Life." *Los Angeles Times*, August 19, 1988.

"Instant Fad." *Time*, October 20, 1961.

Jancik, Wayne. "The Dreamlovers: Keeping the Dream Alive." *Goldmine*, December 28, 1990.

———. "Chubby Checker: Twistin' Time Is Still Here." *Goldmine*, December 28, 1990.

Metz, Robert. "Market Place." *New York Times*, February 24, 1968.

Milewski, Krazy Greg. "You Can't Sit Down." *Cat Tales*, May 1994.

"Moscow Attack on the Twist." *London Times*, April 30, 1962.

"New Oxford Dictionary Doesn't List the Twist." *New York Times*, September 30, 1962.

"Oops." *Newsweek*, January 8, 1962.

Paulsen, Don. "Interview with Sam Cooke." *Rhythm and Blues Magazine*, July 1964.

"Popular Dances From the Cakewalk to the Watusi." *Ebony*, August 1961.

"Remembrance of Things Past." *Newsweek*, January 8, 1962.

"Risk in the Twist Cited by Surgeon." *New York Times*, December 3, 1961.

Rowland, Mark. "Dick Clark." *Sh-Boom*, January 1989.

"Sacroili-act, The." *Newsweek*, December 4, 1961.

"Saigon Regime Bans Songs for Twisting." *New York Times*, April 2, 1963.

Shabad, Theodore. "Poet Tells Soviet Twist Can Be Nice." *New York Times*, May 27, 1962.

Soocher, Stan. "The Royalty Recovery Project." *Musician*, January 1988.

"Soviet Is Seeking a Twist Antidote." *New York Times*, April 5, 1964.

"Suit Is Challenged By Cameo-Parkway." *New York Times*, September 5, 1967.

"Syria Bans the Twist." *London Times*, January 17, 1962.

Talese, Gay. "Twist Danced at Metropolitan As Director Watches in Dismay." *New York Times*, November 21, 1961.

"Talk of the Town." *The New Yorker*, October 21, 1961.

Tamarkin, Jeff. "Dick Clark: The Beat Goes On." *Goldmine*, December 28, 1990.

———. The Hank Ballard Discography. *The Golden Age, No. 8* (booklet), May 1987.

Thompson, Howard. "Producers Rush Movies on Twist." *New York Times*, January 6, 1962.

———. "The Screen: 'Twist Around the Clock'." *New York Times*, January 27, 1962.

Thompson, Robert Farris. "Music in the Market Place." *Saturday Review*, May 26, 1962.

Topping, Seymour. "Soviet Out of Step with Twist." *New York Times*, April 29, 1962.

"Twist Annoys Red China." *New York Times*, September 16, 1962.

"Twist Straightens Up Reds' Inept Workers." *New York Times*, October 27, 1963.

"Twist Wiggles Into Big Time." *Business Week*, December 2, 1961.

"Twisting a Fad for Cash." *Life*, January 12, 1962.

Wehrwein, Austin C. "Eisenhower Discerns a Decline in Morality." *New York Times*, May 2, 1962.

"Work Is Never Play." *Newsweek*, April 9, 1962.

Radio

King of the Queen City: The Story of King Records, produced and written by Jon Hartley Fox.

Let's Twist Again, BBC Radio 2, produced by Keith Locksen, written and presented by Louise Bruce, 1992.

Interviews by Jim Dawson

Phone interviews with Dave Appell, December 3, 1993 and March 12, 1994.

Interviews with Hank Ballard, Los Angeles, 1987; April 13, 1988; July 1, 1994.

Interview with Richard Berry, Los Angeles, January 19, 1994.

Phone interview with Freddy Cannon, September 14, 1994.

Phone interviews with Joe Cook, June 2, 1988; February 9, 1994.

Phone interview with Joey Dee, January 9, 1994.

Phone interview with Charlie Gracie, December 1, 1993.

Interview with Cal Green, Los Angeles, June 5, 1988.

Phone interview with Gladys Horton, March 12, 1994.

Phone interview with Kal Mann, December 5, 1993.

Phone interview with John Medora, February 25, 1994.

Phone interview with Bobby Robinson, March 1993.

Phone interviews with Chuck Rubin, August 25, 1993, and September 16, 1994.

Phone interview with Joseph Wallace, June 9, 1988.

Phone interview with Dave White, February 25, 1994.

Index of Names

About the Author

Although Jim Dawson's teachers and friends routinely assured him that he would never amount to anything, he won a Twist contest in 1961 in his home town of Parkersburg, West Virginia. He has never grown up, which may account for his collection of over twenty thousand rockabilly and R&B recordings from the pre-1962 era. Dawson is the coauthor, with Steve Propes, of Faber and Faber's *What was the First Rock 'n' Roll Record?* and the author of *Nervous Man Nervous*, a history of the classic rhythm and blues tenor saxophonists. He lives in Hollywood, California.